11+ Maths

For GL Assessment

This CGP book is brilliant for children aged 9-10 who are working towards the GL 11+. It's set at a slightly easier level than the real test — perfect for building confidence.

The first few sections are packed with topic-based questions that'll help them get to grips with each crucial skill. Once they've mastered those, they can move on to the mixed-topic Assessment Tests for more realistic 11+ practice.

There are also detailed answers to make marking as simple as possible!

How to access your free Online Edition

This book includes a free Online Edition to read on your PC, Mac or tablet.
You'll just need to go to cgpbooks.co.uk/extras and enter this code:

4051 3533 1973 2562

By the way, this code only works for one person. If somebody else has used this book before you, they might have already claimed the Online Edition.

Practice Book – Ages 9-10

with Assessment Tests

How to use this Practice Book

This book is divided into two parts — themed question practice and assessment tests. There are answers and detailed explanations at the back of the book.

Themed question practice

- Each page contains practice questions divided by topic. Use these pages to work out your child's strengths and the areas they find tricky. The questions get harder down each page.

- Your child can use the smiley face tick boxes to evaluate how confident they feel with each topic.

Assessment tests

- The second half of the book contains five assessment tests, each with a mix of question types from the first half of the book. They take a similar form to the real test.

- You can print multiple-choice answer sheets so your child can practise the tests as if they're sitting the real thing — visit cgpbooks.co.uk/11plus/answer-sheets or scan the QR code.

Answer Sheets

- Use the printable answer sheets if you want your child to do each test more than once.

- If you want to give your child timed practice, give them a time limit of 40 minutes for each test, and ask them to work as quickly and carefully as they can.

- Your child should aim for a mark of around 85% (34 questions correct) in each test. If they score less than this, use their results to work out the areas they need more practice on.

- If they haven't managed to finish the test in time, they need to work on increasing their speed, whereas if they have made a lot of mistakes, they need to work more carefully.

- Keep track of your child's scores using the progress chart at the back of the book.

Published by CGP

Editors:
Luke Antieul, Joe Brazier, David Broadbent, Megan Tyler, Sarah Williams

Contributors:
John Davis, Cynthia Deeson, Sumyya Hassan, John Hawkins

With thanks to Simon Greaves and Rosie McCurrie for the proofreading.

Please note that CGP is not associated with GL Assessment in any way. This book does not include any official questions and is not endorsed by GL Assessment

ISBN: 978 1 78908 158 9
Printed by Bell & Bain Ltd, Glasgow.
Clipart from Corel®

Based on the classic CGP style created by Richard Parsons.

Text, design, layout and original illustrations © Coordination Group Publications Ltd. (CGP) 2018
All rights reserved.

Photocopying this book is not permitted, even if you have a CLA licence.
Extra copies are available from CGP with next day delivery • 0800 1712 712 • www.cgpbooks.co.uk

Contents

Tick off the check box for each topic as you go along.

Section One — Number Knowledge

Place Value .... 2 ✓
Rounding Up and Down 3
Number Knowledge 4
Number Sequences 6
Fractions 7
Ratio and Proportion 8
Percentages, Fractions
and Decimals 9

Section Two — Working with Numbers

Addition 10
Subtraction 11
Multiplying and Dividing
by 10, 100 and 1000 12
Multiplication 13
Division 15
Algebra 16

Section Three — Number Problems

Mixed Calculations 17
Word Problems 18

Section Four — Data Handling

Data Tables 20
Displaying Data 21
The Mean 23

Section Five — Shape and Space

Angles 24
2D Shapes 25
2D Shapes — Perimeter and Area .. 27
Symmetry 29
3D Shapes 30
Shape Problems 32
Coordinates 33

Section Six — Units and Measures

Units 35
Time 37

Section Seven — Mixed Problems

Mixed Problems 39

Assessment Tests

Test 1 41
Test 2 46
Test 3 52
Test 4 57
Test 5 62

Answers 67
Progress Chart 94

Section One — Number Knowledge

Place Value

Write down the place value of each digit underlined below.

1. 1<u>6</u>3.92   Answer: _____
2. <u>3</u>780.3   Answer: _____
3. 298.0<u>3</u>9   Answer: _____
4. 72 636.<u>4</u>8   Answer: _____
5. 5591.28<u>1</u>   Answer: _____

/ 5

Circle the smallest number in each row below.

6. 16.2   32.9   84.9   172.3   1.62
7. 32.4   30.2   302   3.02   32.0
8. 123.7   132.7   312.7   127.3   317.2
9. 1.35   1.27   1.61   1.84   1.37
10. 1.044   0.144   10.44   0.441   1.444

Hint: You need to look at the place value of the digits to work out which number is the smallest.

/ 5

11. What is eight million, seventeen thousand four hundred and fifty-two in figures?   Answer: _____

Write down the number the arrow is pointing to on each of the number lines below.

12. 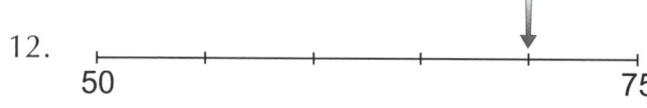   Answer: _____

13.    Answer: _____

14. The table on the right shows the results of the Class 5B 80 m race. Who came last?

    Answer: _____

Name	Time (seconds)
Jake	14.36
Holly	13.59
Jack	14.4
Micah	13.5
Olivia	14.04

15. Which of these pairs of numbers are the same distance from 5?

    5.19 and 4.91
    5.11 and 4.99
    5.11 and 4.91
    5.11 and 4.89
    5.01 and 4.91   Answer: _____

/ 5

Rounding Up and Down

Round the following numbers.

1. 786 to the nearest 10   Answer: _____
2. 851 to the nearest 100   Answer: _____
3. 2421 to the nearest 100   Answer: _____
4. 8578 to the nearest 1000   Answer: _____
5. 4426 to the nearest 1000   Answer: _____

/ 5

Write down whether each of the numbers below have been rounded to the nearest 10, 100 or 1000.

6. 355 rounded to 400   Answer: _____
7. 278 rounded to 280   Answer: _____
8. 3682 rounded to 3680   Answer: _____
9. 4367 rounded to 4000   Answer: _____
10. 3469 rounded to 3500   Answer: _____

/ 5

11. Round 27 642 to the nearest 100.   Answer: _____

12. Round 175.639 to the nearest whole number.   Answer: _____

13. An apple weighs 100.364 grams.
    Round this weight to the nearest tenth of a gram.   Answer: _____ g

14. Matt is 159.67 cm tall. What is Matt's height rounded to the nearest whole centimetre? Circle the correct answer.

    152 cm   157 cm   160 cm   150 cm   159 cm

15. Which of the options below will equal 1000?
    A 1652 rounded to the nearest 1000
    B 847 rounded to the nearest 100
    C 956 rounded to the nearest 100
    D 987 rounded to the nearest 10
    E 1239 rounded to the nearest 100   Answer: _____

/ 5

Section One — Number Knowledge

Number Knowledge

Circle the smallest number in each row below.

1. 5   −2   0.5   −5   2.5
2. −9   −7   7   −1   9
3. −1   −18   −10   0   −28
4. −20   −30   −24   −26   −22
5. −1   1.5   0.1   0.05   0.15

/ 5

Choose one number from this list of numbers to fill in the gaps below.

    −13   6.5   20   6.65   −7   64.5   22   −11   21   98

6. _____ > 68

7. 65 > _____ > 64

8. 20 < _____ < 22

9. −12 < _____ < −8

10. 6.9 > _____ > 6.5

Hint: < means 'is less than' and > means 'is greater than'.

/ 5

11. Which number is in the wrong place on this Venn diagram? Circle the correct answer.

   A 7   C 64   E 28
   B 12   D 21

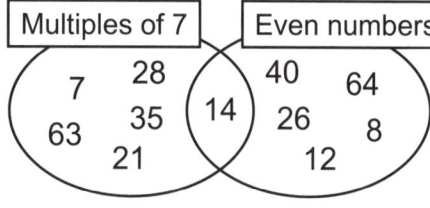

12. Circle the statement which is incorrect.

   −5 < 8 − 10   −3 > −7 + 3   6 > −3 + 9   −4 > 3 − 8   −1 = 3 − 4

13. Which of the numbers below is a multiple of 3 and 4? Circle the correct answer.

      15   16   18   24   32

14. Kat throws three darts. The total score of the three darts has to be an even number for her to win the game. Which set of dart scores would not give her a winning total? Circle the correct answer.

   A 34, 28, 12   C 60, 54, 8   E 22, 48, 36
   B 33, 27, 50   D 13, 21, 57

15. Darren thinks of a number and cubes it. The answer is 19 less than the next cube number. Circle the number Darren was thinking of.

   A 2   B 3   C 4   D 9   E 10

16. Which of these numbers is a common factor of 18 and 24? Circle the correct answer.

      4   5   6   8   9

/ 6

Section One — Number Knowledge

Number Knowledge

17. What is the sum of all the prime numbers between 1 and 10?   Answer: _____

18. Sara adds five to the largest prime number below 20.
    What answer should she get?   Answer: _____

19. The table on the right has been filled in incorrectly. Which row is the only row that has been filled in correctly?

    Answer: _____

Row	Prime Number	Square number	Multiple of 6
A	25	19	12
B	21	16	32
C	27	25	24
D	29	30	66
E	29	36	42

20. Which of these numbers would go into the shaded section of the Venn diagram?

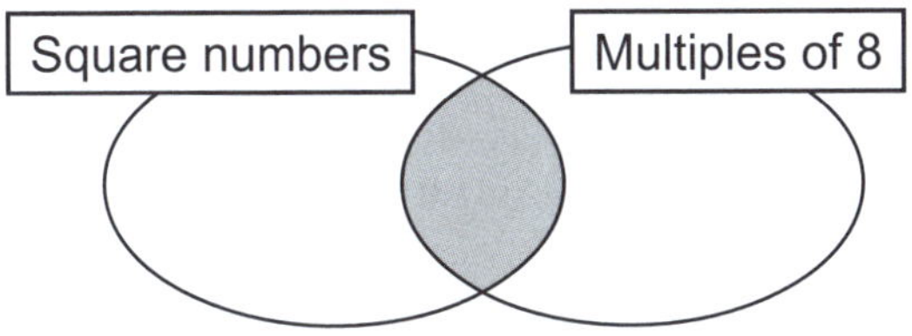

    A 1 and 9
    B 16 and 25
    C 16 and 64
    D 25 and 64
    E 36 and 64   Answer: _____

21. Which of the following lists of numbers would go into the empty box in this sorting diagram?

    A 3, 5, 9, 11
    B 3, 11, 27, 31
    C 5, 8, 12, 14
    D 9, 13, 18, 21
    E 9, 15, 21, 33   Answer: _____

	Prime	Not Prime
Even	2	4, 10, 12, 28
Odd	7, 11, 13, 19	

22. Lucy drew this sorting diagram. Her teacher pointed out that one number can go in two places in the diagram. Which number is it? Circle the correct answer.

    1   6   5   3   9

	Factor of 18	Prime
< 10		
> 10		

23. Which of these multiples of 3 add up to make a factor of 36?

    A 3 and 12
    B 6 and 21
    C 3 and 15
    D 6 and 27
    E 9 and 12   Answer: _____

24. Amy is 3^2 years old and her grandma is 8^2 years old.
    What is the difference between their ages?   Answer: _____ years

25. The year Bodhi was born is represented by the Roman numeral MCMXLIX.
    What year was Bodhi born?

    A 1946   B 1954   C 1969   D 1949   E 1964

Number Sequences

Write down the missing number in each gap in the sequences below.

1. 8   16   24   32   _____   4. 48   60   72   84   _____
2. 27   24   21   18   _____   5. 2   20   200   2000 _____
3. 11   33   55   77   _____

  / 5

Write down the fourth number in the sequence which follows each rule below.

6. Start at 1, count on in steps of 3.   Answer: _____
7. Start at 1, double the previous number.   Answer: _____
8. Start at –3, count on in steps of 2.   Answer: _____
9. Start at 20, count back in steps of 8.   Answer: _____
10. Start at 2.5, count on in steps of 2.5.   Answer: _____

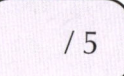 / 5

11. Chris is building a tower out of rectangular blocks. The tower has 3 rows and there are 9 blocks on the bottom row. How many blocks would there be on the bottom row of a tower with 6 rows?

    Answer: _____

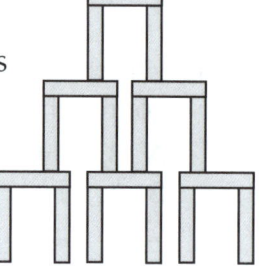

12. Polly starts with a number between 5 and 10. She counts up in steps of 5 until she reaches 38. What number did she start off with?   Answer: _____

13. Ashley started at the number 3 and made a sequence by doubling the number each time. Which of these numbers were in her sequence? Circle the correct answer.

    A 9, 30   B 15, 48   C 12, 36   D 20, 38   E 12, 48

14. Amira writes the following sequence on the whiteboard, but rubs out the first and last numbers:

    ____   1.75   2.5   3.25   4   ____

    What are the missing numbers? Circle the correct answer.

    0.5 and 4.75   0 and 5   1 and 4.75   1.5 and 5.5   0.75 and 5.25

15. Mrs Roberts feeds her dogs 3 tins of dog food each day. After feeding her dogs on Monday, Mrs Roberts has 13 tins of dog food left. Which day will this food run out? Circle the correct answer.

    Wednesday   Thursday   Friday   Saturday   Sunday

  / 5

Section One — Number Knowledge

Fractions

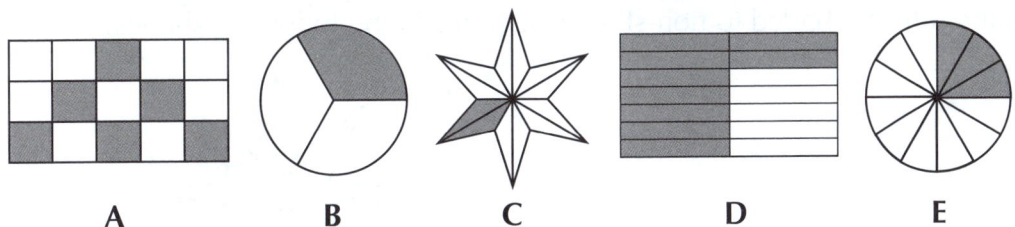

A   B   C   D   E

A fraction of each of these shapes is shaded. Write down the letter of the shape which has each of the following fractions shaded.

1. 1/3   Answer: _____
2. 1/4   Answer: _____
3. 9/14   Answer: _____
4. 6/15   Answer: _____
5. 1/6   Answer: _____

/ 5

A tin contains 24 biscuits and is shared between 5 people.
Write down how many biscuits each person gets.

6. Dan's share is 1/6 of the biscuits.   Answer: _____
7. Ally's share is 1/4 of the biscuits.   Answer: _____
8. Molly's share is 1/12 of the biscuits.   Answer: _____
9. George's share is 1/8 of the biscuits.   Answer: _____
10. Maya's share is 3/8 of the biscuits.   Answer: _____

/ 5

11. Joe, Marcus, Alan and John put together their spending money to buy a box of 12 doughnuts. They receive another box of twelve doughnuts for free. If they divided the doughnuts equally, what fraction of the total number of doughnuts should each boy receive? Circle the correct answer.

    A 4/12   B 12/24   C 4/24   D 1/4   E 6/12

12. Circle the largest fraction.

    1/2   5/12   2/3   5/6   1/3

13. How many fifths are there in 11? Circle the correct answer.

    11   15   22   34   55

14. Lisa is painting her fence. Her fence has 18 posts. Lisa paints 1/3 of them red. How many posts were not painted red?   Answer: _____

15. The local library's membership is made up of 50 women and 40 men. What fraction of the total membership is made up of men? Circle the correct answer.

    1/40   4/5   40/50   5/4   4/9

/ 5

Section One — Number Knowledge

Ratio and Proportion

What is the ratio of shaded to non-shaded sections in the following shapes?

1. 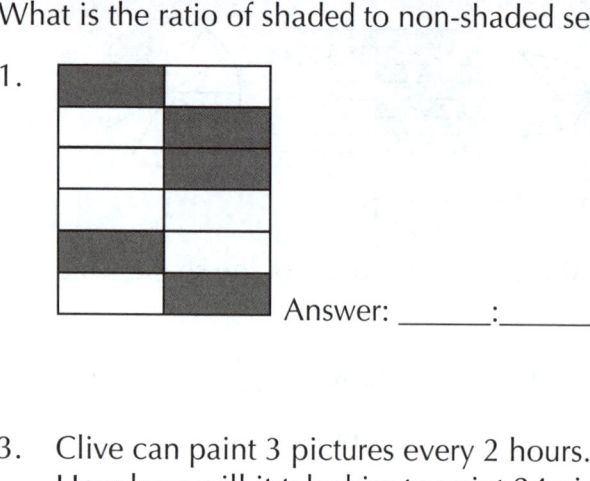 Answer: _____ : _____

2. 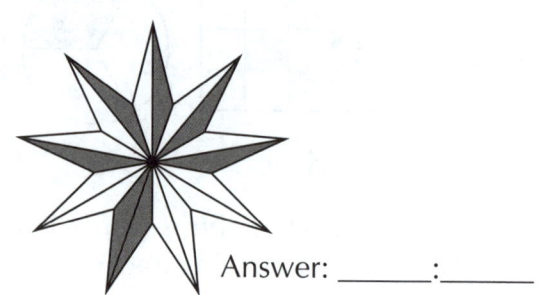 Answer: _____ : _____

3. Clive can paint 3 pictures every 2 hours.
   How long will it take him to paint 24 pictures?   Answer: _____ hours

4. While walking to school, Andreas found that 1 in every 9 cars
   that drove by him were red. 8 red cars drove by him.
   What was the total number of cars that drove by Andreas?

   Answer: _____ cars

/ 4

Divide 48 into the following ratios.

Hint: Add up the numbers in the ratio to find the total number of parts, then find the size of one part.

5. 1:3   Answer: _____ : _____

6. 5:1   Answer: _____ : _____

7. 3:5   Answer: _____ : _____

8. 1:11 Answer: _____ : _____

9. 2:1   Answer: _____ : _____

10. 13:3 Answer: _____ : _____

/ 6

11. A recipe to make 8 cupcakes requires 4 eggs, 250 grams of flour,
    300 grams of butter and 350 grams of sugar.
    How many cupcakes would 900 grams of butter make?

    Answer: _____ cupcakes

12. A zookeeper is counting the animals in the reptile house.
    He counts 11 snakes and finds that there are 5 more lizards than snakes.
    What is the ratio of snakes to lizards?

    Answer: _____ : _____

/ 2

Section One — Number Knowledge

Percentages, Fractions and Decimals

Fill in the missing percentage, fraction (in its simplest form) or decimal in each row.

	Percentage %	Fraction	Decimal
1.	50	½	
2.	30		0.3
3.		¾	0.75
4.	20	⅕	
5.		⅗	0.6

/ 5

Kelly's favourite clothes shop has a sale. Work out the sale prices of these items:

6. A shirt which originally cost £12 with 50% off. Answer: £ _____

7. A pair of jeans which originally cost £20 with 20% off. Answer: £ _____

8. A leather jacket which originally cost £40 with 25% off. Answer: £ _____

9. A hat and a pair of gloves which originally cost £8 with 10% off. Answer: £ _____

10. A pair of stripy socks which originally cost £4 with 5% off. Answer: £ _____

/ 5

11. Sasha's dog had a litter of 10 puppies. Three were black and the rest were brown. What percentage of the puppies were brown? Answer: _____ %

12. 15% of a 50 gram chocolate bar is cocoa. How many grams is this? Answer: _____ g

13. Class 5K recorded the hair colour of every pupil in their class and put the results into a pie chart. What fraction of the pupils had red hair? Circle the correct answer.

    A ⅕   B ¹⁄₁₀   C ⅛   D ⅙   E ²⁄₉

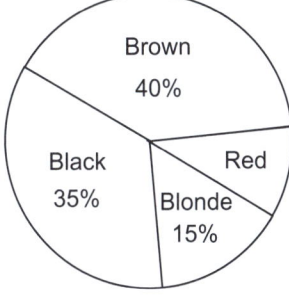

14. Circle the calculation which gives the smallest answer.

    ¼ of 100   75% of 80   50% of 60   ⅗ of 25   25% of 40

15. Circle the statement which is correct.

    A ⅕ > 0.2   B ½ = 0.2   C 0.35 > ¼   D ⁶⁄₁₀ = 0.65   E ⅖ > 0.5

/ 5

Section One — Number Knowledge

Section Two — Working with Numbers

Addition

Look at the menu on the right and work out how much it would cost to buy the following items:

Menu
Sandwich £2.00
Teacake £1.35
Scone £1.85
Tea £1.40
Coffee £1.25
Orange juice £1.50

1. A sandwich and an orange juice.   Answer: £ _____
2. Tea and a teacake.   Answer: £ _____
3. Coffee and a scone.   Answer: £ _____
4. Orange juice and a scone.   Answer: £ _____
5. A scone and a teacake.   Answer: £ _____

/ 5

Work out the answer to each calculation.

6. 428 + 23   Answer: _____
7. 6.4 + 3.7   Answer: _____
8. 8.5 + 16.3   Answer: _____
9. 12.5 + 26.7   Answer: _____
10. 12.5 + 3.72   Answer: _____

Hint: If you add the decimals using the column method, remember to line up the decimal points.

/ 5

11. Rebecca buys one kilogram of apples, one and a half kilograms of pears, half a kilogram of oranges, and half a kilogram of onions.
    How much does her shopping weigh altogether?   Answer: _____ kg

12. Jamie is 147 cm tall, Micky is 149 cm and Kyle is 151 cm.
    What is the total height of the three boys in centimetres?   Answer: _____ cm

13. Latisha has a 50p coin, six 20p coins, a 5p coin and four 2p coins.
    How much money does she have in pounds?   Answer: £ _____

14. The maximum weight of people allowed in one log on a log flume ride is 250 kg.
    The four members of Farida's family weigh 79 kg, 55 kg, 42 kg and 37 kg.
    Circle the true statement below.

    A Farida's family can sit together in one log because their total weight is below 200 kg.
    B Farida's family can sit together in one log because their total weight is around 215 kg.
    C Farida's family can sit together in one log because their total weight is 245 kg.
    D Farida's family cannot sit together in one log because their total weight is around 215 kg.
    E Farida's family cannot sit together in one log because their total weight is over 250 kg.

15. On the day of the school fair, Mrs Baker used 31.5 litres of water to make tea, 20.75 litres of water for coffee and 30.25 litres for squash. How much water was used in total to make these drinks?

    Answer: _____ litres

/ 5

Subtraction

Work out the answer to each calculation.

Hint: One way of tackling subtraction calculations is to use partitioning. But sometimes it's quicker to use a different method, such as counting up.

1. 76 − 25   Answer: _____

2. 67 − 18   Answer: _____

3. 112 − 83   Answer: _____

4. 120 − 103   Answer: _____

5. 18.3 − 12.6   Answer: _____

/ 5

Work out how much change you would receive from a £5 note if you spent the following amounts:

6. £3.55   Answer: £ _____

7. 89p   Answer: £ _____

8. £4.37   Answer: £ _____

9. £2.08   Answer: £ _____

10. £1.11   Answer: £ _____

/ 5

11. Sam is going on holiday. His suitcase can carry 25 kg. If he has already packed 15.7 kg, what is the maximum weight he can add to his suitcase? Circle the correct answer.

    A 9.7 kg   **B** 9.3 kg   **C** 12.8 kg   **D** 10.3 kg   **E** 8.7 kg

12. What is 2 − 1.78?   Answer: _____

13. Frankie had £20.35. He bought a football magazine for £1.80 and an ice cream for £1.25. How much money did he have left?

    Answer: £ _____

14. The maximum temperature on Monday was −6 °C. On Tuesday the maximum temperature was 2 °C. What was the difference between the maximum temperatures on Monday and Tuesday?

    Answer: _____ °C

15. Daisy fills a jug with 3 litres of orange juice. She pours 0.56 litres of orange juice into one glass and 0.3 litres into another. How much orange juice is left in the jug?

    Answer: _____ litres

/ 5

Section Two — Working with Numbers

Multiplying and Dividing by 10, 100 and 1000

Write down the answer to each calculation.

1. 27 × 100   Answer: _____

2. 350 × 10   Answer: _____

3. 7.84 × 100   Answer: _____

4. 65.5 × 10   Answer: _____

5. 0.4 × 1000   Answer: _____

/ 5

Complete the table below.

	Number	Divided by 10	Divided by 100	Divided by 1000
6.	43 000	4300	430	
7.	3672		36.72	3.672
8.	5050	505		5.05
9.	23		0.23	0.023
10.	8.5	0.85		0.0085

/ 5

11. Cecil charges 85p for one iced cupcake. If he sells 100 cupcakes, how much money will he receive in pounds?

    Answer: £ _____

12. There are 1548 children at Dinah's school. Homework planners come in boxes of 10. How many boxes should the school order so that there are enough homework planners for every child to have one?

    Answer: _____

13. Patrick thinks of a number. He first multiplies it by 10 and then divides his answer by 1000. He ends up with 1.3. What number did he start off with?

    Answer: _____

14. 1250 = 1000 × ____

    What number is missing from the equation above? Circle the correct answer.

    125   125 000   12 500   1.25   12.5

15. 1283 _____ = 0.1283 × 100

    Which of the following should go in the gap in the equation above? Circle the correct answer.

    A × 10   B × 100   C × 1000   D ÷ 100   E ÷ 1000

/ 5

Section Two — Working with Numbers

Multiplication

A number machine multiplies numbers by 12.
What number comes out when the following numbers are put in?

Hint: You can partition 12 into 10 and 2.

1. 9 → × 12 → Answer: _____
2. 12 → Answer: _____
3. 15 → Answer: _____
4. 20 → Answer: _____
5. 400 → Answer: _____

/ 5

Work out the answer to each calculation.

6. 36 × 5   Answer: _____
7. 19 × 4   Answer: _____
8. 3 × 1.5   Answer: _____
9. 6 × 3.5   Answer: _____
10. 2.25 × 4 Answer: _____

/ 5

11. Bella buys 5 chewy bars at 29p each. What is the total cost in pounds?

    Answer: £ _____

12. Zac buys 3 packets of crisp at 45p each and 4 toffee crunches at 25p each. What is the total cost in pounds?

    Answer: £ _____

13. 1 measure of car shampoo must be diluted with 6 measures of water. How much water should be added to 120 ml of car shampoo?   Answer: _____ ml

14. Which of the following is equal to 12.6 × 5.5? Circle the correct answer.

    A 0.0693   C 6.93   E 693
    B 0.693   D 69.3

    Hint: Use rounding to estimate the answer.

15. 420 + 420 + 420 + 420 + 420 + 420 = 12 × _____
    Circle the missing number.

    A 210   B 105   C 52.5   D 840   E 26.25

16. 250 × 8 = 2000

    What is 250 × 0.008?   Answer: _____

/ 6

Section Two — Working with Numbers

Multiplication

17. $75 \times 231 = 17\,325$

    What is 75×462? Circle the correct answer.

    A 346 500 B 3465 C 35 000 D 34 650 E 34 000

18. Sarah buys a comic costing £1.50 each month.
    How much does Sarah spend on comics in three years?   Answer: £ _____

19. Three friends hire bikes for £5.50 per hour. If the friends
    use the bikes for four hours, what will their total bill be?   Answer: £ _____

20. $4.3 \times 3.8 = 16.34$

    What is 43×0.38? Circle the correct answer.

    A 1634 B 163.4 C 16.34 D 1.634 E 0.1634

21. Iqbal buys 26 pens for 98p each and 11 rulers for £1.49 each.
    Which of these calculations give the total cost? Circle the correct answer.

    A 26 × £1 − 26p + 11 × £1.50 − 11p
    B 26 × £1 + 52p + 11 × £1.50 + 11p
    C 26 × 98p − 52p + 11 × £1.49 − 11p
    D 26 × £1 − 52p + 11 × £1.50 − 11p
    E 11 × £1 − 2p + 26 × £1.50 − 1p

22. What is 0.7×0.8?   Answer: _____

    Hint: Use the answer to 7 × 8 to help you work out 0.7 × 0.8.

23. $2025 = 45 \times 45$

    Which of the following calculations is equal to 4050? Circle the correct answer.

    A 90 × 90
    B 45 × 45 × 45
    C 90 × 45
    D 90 × 22.5
    E 22.5 × 45

24. Packs of 4 toilet rolls are on offer and cost 80p each.
    Mr Lewis wants to stock up but only has £10.
    How many toilet rolls can he buy?

    Hint: Read the question carefully. It asks for the number of rolls, not the number of packs.

    Answer: _____

     /8

Division

Work out the answer to each calculation.

1. 48 ÷ 8   Answer: _____
2. 56 ÷ 7   Answer: _____
3. 72 ÷ 9   Answer: _____
4. 66 ÷ 6   Answer: _____
5. 51 ÷ 3   Answer: _____

/ 5

Adam, Amy and Alfie are triplets. On their birthday, they were given some amounts of money to share equally. Work out how much money each triplet receives from each person.

6. Their grandma gave them £60.   Answer: £ _____
7. Their uncle gave them £45.   Answer: £ _____
8. Their mother gave them £99.   Answer: £ _____
9. Their brother gave them £9.99.   Answer: £ _____
10. Their aunt gave them £10.50.   Answer: £ _____

/ 5

11. Salima's hens lay 40 eggs each week. She packs them into boxes that each hold 6 eggs. How many boxes does she use each week?   Answer: _____

12. Adil paid £72 for four terms of swimming lessons. What is the cost for each term of lessons?   Answer: £ _____

13. Jason shares a bag of biscuits equally between seven dogs. There are some biscuits left over. Which of these numbers cannot be the number of biscuits left over? Circle the correct answer.

    A 7   B 6   C 5   D 4   E 3

14. Sharon needs 132 m of wire fencing to go around her garden to keep cats out. The fencing comes in 8 m rolls. How many rolls of fencing does she need? Circle the correct answer.

    A 10   C 20   E 16
    B 17   D 19

15. Jane's wedding cake has a weight of 1600 g. The cake is cut into slices weighing 40 g each. How many slices are there?

    Answer: _____

/ 5

Section Two — Working with Numbers

Algebra

If $a = 4$, work out the value of the following expressions.

1. $56 - a$ Answer: _____
2. $73 + a$ Answer: _____
3. $6a$ Answer: _____
4. $32 \div a$ Answer: _____
5. $3a - 2$ Answer: _____

Hint: If a number and a letter are next to each other, you need to multiply them together.

The expression $3n - 1$ can be used to find the nth term in a number sequence. Use the expression to find each of the following terms in the sequence.

6. The 1st term. Answer: _____
7. The 6th term. Answer: _____
8. The 10th term. Answer: _____
9. The 15th term. Answer: _____
10. The 20th term. Answer: _____

Hint: To find a term, replace n in $3n - 1$ with the term number and work out the calculation.

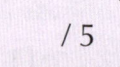

11. A bouncy castle company uses the formula $25 + 7z$ to work out how many pounds to charge people when they hire a bouncy castle for z hours. If Mrs Shah wants to hire a bouncy castle for 5 hours, how much will she be charged?

Hint: Use the BODMAS rule — do multiplication before addition.

Answer: £ _____

12. A football club are ordering kits for the new season. The cost, in pounds, of y kits is given by the expression $15 + 8y$. How much will it cost the club if they order 20 kits?

Answer: £ _____

13. Gaby is x years old. Her mum is 24 years older. Which expression gives Gaby's mum's age in years? Circle the correct answer.

   A $x - 24$ **B** $x + 24$ **C** $24x$ **D** $24 - x$ **E** $24 \div x$

14. Mr Ali is ordering some Maths books over the Internet. The books cost £3 each and the postage is £4.99 for an order of any size. Which expression gives the cost, in pounds, of ordering y books? Circle the correct answer.

   A $3y + 4.99y$ **C** $3 + 4.99y$ **E** $3y + 4.99$
   B $3y$ **D** $3y - 4.99$

Section Two — Working with Numbers

Section Three — Number Problems

Mixed Calculations

Write down the answer to each calculation.

1. (37 + 13) × 3   Answer: _____

2. 56 + (29 − 17)   Answer: _____

3. 150 ÷ (18 + 12)   Answer: _____

4. 235 − (3 × 7)   Answer: _____

Hint: Work out the part of each calculation in brackets first.

/ 4

The table shows the prices charged at a play centre. Answer the following questions.

Entry Prices	Baby (Age 6 to 12 months)	£1.50
	Toddler (Age 1 to 3 years)	£2.25
	Child (Age 3 to 14 years)	£3.25
Extras	Go Kart ride	£1.50
	Snack Pack	£1.00

5. How much would entry for one toddler and two children cost?

   Answer: £ _____

6. Three 14 year olds each pay for entry to the play centre and a Go Kart ride. Which of these calculations could be used to work out the total amount they paid? Circle the correct answer.

   A 3 × 2.25 + 3 × 1.00   C 3.25 + 3 × 1.50   E 3 × 3.25 + 3 × 1.50
   B 3 × 3.25 + 1.50   D 3 × 1.50 + 3 × 1.00

7. David buys entry for two children and pays for two Go Kart rides and two Snack Packs. How much change will he receive from a £20 note?

   Answer: £ _____

/ 3

8. What is 79 × 365 + 365 × 21? Circle the correct answer.

   830   1730   19 989   36 500   73 000

9. Which of these calculations does not equal 81? Circle the correct answer.

   A 39 + 25 × 2 − 8   C 21 + 100 ÷ 2 + 10   E 10 × 5 + 8 + 23
   B 50 + 31 × 1   D 50 × 10 + 39 − 8

10. What is 2.5 × 8 − 12?   Answer: _____

11. Which calculation has the largest value? Circle the correct answer.

    A 10 × 9 + 8 − 7   C 9 × 10 + 7 − 8   E 7 × 9 + 8 − 10
    B 10 × 7 + 9 − 8   D 8 × 7 + 10 − 9

12. Max needs the ingredients shown to make 12 fairy cakes. He wants to make 18 fairy cakes instead of 12. How much sugar will he need to use?

    Answer: _____ g

Fairy Cakes (makes 12)
250 g flour
250 g sugar
250 g butter
2 eggs

/ 5

Word Problems

1. One banana and three mangos cost £2.30. The banana costs 80p. How much does one mango cost?   Answer: _____ p

2. Dina bought five different pairs of shoes that cost £25.00 each. She decided to keep two pairs and returned the others. How much money was she refunded for the shoes she returned?   Answer: £ _____

3. Arya's gerbil has 20 g of food each day. Each packet of food contains 250 g. Arya buys four packets. How many days will this food last?   Answer: _____

4. Mrs Cooper fills her car up with diesel. She pays with two £20 notes and receives £11.63 change. How much did the fuel for the car cost?   Answer: £ _____

5. Henry has £1.60 to buy stationery for school. Which of these does he have exactly the right amount of money to buy? Circle the correct answer.

Pens	70p each
Pencils	55p each
Rubbers	35p each

   A 2 pencils and 1 rubber
   B 3 pencils
   C 1 pen and 2 rubbers
   D 1 pencil, 1 rubber and 1 pen
   E 1 pencil, 2 rubbers and 1 pen

6. Esther made an apple cake and a carrot cake of the same size. The apple cake was divided into 12 equal slices and the carrot cake was divided into 6 equal slices. At a cake sale, Esther sold 4 slices of apple cake and 4 slices of carrot cake. Which of these statements is correct? Circle the correct answer.

   A The same amount of both cakes was sold.
   B ½ of the carrot cake was sold.
   C ¼ of the apple cake was sold.
   D More of the apple cake was sold than the carrot cake.
   E In total 1 whole cake was sold.

   Hint: Start by working out the fraction of each cake that was sold.

7. A shop pays £15.00 for 20 kg of potatoes. They charge customers £1.20 per kilogram of potatoes. If the shop sells all of the potatoes, what will be the difference between the amount of money they spent and the amount of money they earned selling potatoes? Circle the correct answer.

   A £15   B £9   C £16   D £12   E £20

8. Zac and Isa are making party bags for 13 children. They put three different toys into each bag. The toys come in packs of nine. How many packs will Zac and Isa need to buy?

   Answer: _____

9. A clothes shop has a sale. The price of every item is reduced by half every week. A jacket that had originally cost £148 has now been reduced to £18.50. How many weeks has the jacket been in the sale? Circle the correct answer.

   A 3   B 2   C 7   D 5   E 4

Word Problems

10. Alexa is making bracelets. She needs 10 beads and a wire strip for each bracelet. The beads cost 45p each, and the wire costs 75p a strip. How much will it cost her to make three bracelets?

    Answer: £ _____

11. Cameron makes a tower using the 10p coins in his money box. Each 10p coin is 2 mm thick and the tower is 13 cm high. What is the total value of the 10p coins in the tower?

    Answer: £ _____

12. Oliver buys one of each thing on the menu. How much change will Oliver receive from £15?

    Answer: £ _____

1 scoop of ice cream	£1.75
2 scoops of ice cream	£3.25
Ice cream sandwich	£3.45
Slush drink	£1.99

13. Grace has enough space on her MP3 player to store 45 minutes of music. Each song is between 2 minutes and 3 minutes long. What is the minimum number of songs she will be able to store? Circle the correct answer.

    A 22   B 12   C 25   D 15   E 9

14. Ant thinks of a number. He doubles the number and then multiplies the answer by itself. He then adds 15 and is left with 51. What number did he start with?

    Answer: _____

15. A supermarket sells a pack of four peppers for £1.80 or a pack of six peppers for £2.52. What is the cheapest amount you could pay per pepper?

    Answer: _____ p

16. Mr Habib plants 55 bulbs in his garden ready for Spring. They are a mixture of daffodils and tulips. Circle the statement that cannot be true.

    A There are 5 fewer tulips than daffodils.
    B There are 13 more daffodils than tulips.
    C There are more daffodils than tulips.
    D There are 8 more tulips than daffodils.
    E There are more tulips than daffodils.

17. Laura is buying cakes for 20 people. She decides to buy enough cakes so that each person can have one cupcake and half of a doughnut. How much will she spend altogether on the cakes?

Cupcakes	15p each
Doughnuts	52p each
Muffins	24p each

    Answer: £ _____

    / 8

Section Three — Number Problems

Section Four — Data Handling

Data Tables

This table shows the scores of five children in a spelling test. The test was out of 50.

George	Paula	Sanjay	Kate	Nina
37	19	25	39	43

1. Who scored the highest mark?   Answer: _____

2. Find the difference for the scores in the spelling test for Nina and Paula.   Answer: _____

3. Who scored exactly 20 less than Kate?   Answer: _____

4. How many marks did George lose?   Answer: _____

/ 4

The table below shows part of a train timetable for a train running between Appleford and Banbridge.

	Train A	Train B	Train C	Train D
Depart Appleford	09:00	10:30	12:00	14:30
Arrive in Banbridge	11:15	12:00	14:45	16:15

5. Which train takes the longest time?   Answer: _____

6. Which train takes the shortest time?   Answer: _____

7. Robert has to be in Banbridge by 12:15. What is the latest train that he could catch from Appleford?   Answer: _____

/ 3

8. The table shows the finishing times of six children in the 50 m sprint race at sports day. Which child came in third place?

Child	Alan	Marg	Carol	Ranjit	Ahmed	Louisa
Time (secs)	12.8	14.5	15.3	16.2	10.9	11.1

Answer: _____

9. The table shows the number of points scored by archers in a competition. Which of these statements is true? Circle the correct answer.

   A 18 archers scored more than 15 points.
   B Half of the archers scored between 11 and 15 points.
   C 20 archers scored between 0 and 10 points.
   D Less than half the archers scored between 6 and 20 points.
   E 60 archers took part in the competition.

Points scored	Frequency
0 - 5	9
6 - 10	12
11 - 15	19
16 - 20	13
21 - 25	5

10. Kylie is ordering some cakes. She has only filled in some parts of the order form.

Cake	Quantity	Price	Total
Lemon Drizzle	2	£2.00	£4.00
Victoria Sponge	1	£1.50	
Fruit Cake		£3.00	
		Total	£11.50

How many fruit cakes has Kylie ordered?

Answer: _____

/ 3

Displaying Data

The bar chart shows the number of children in five classes.

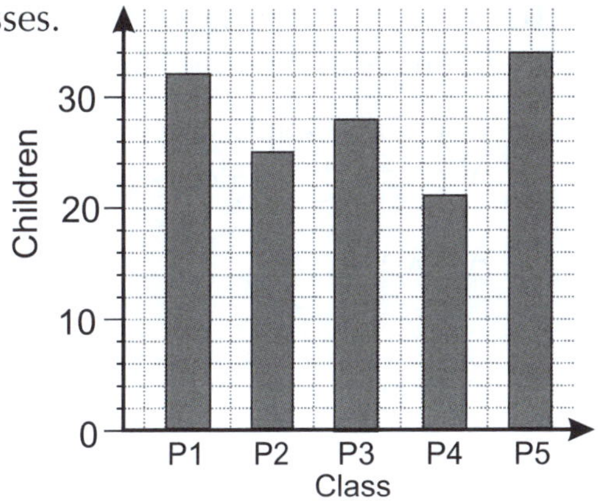

1. Which class has the fewest children in?

    Answer: _____

2. How many children are there in class P2?

    Answer: _____

3. Which two classes have more than 28 children?

    Answer: _____ and _____

4. How many more children are there in P3 than P4?

    Answer: _____

Hint: Read across from the top of a bar to the vertical axis to find out how many children it shows.

/ 4

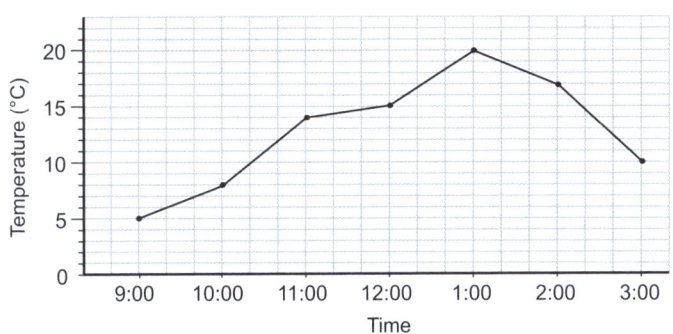

This line graph shows the temperature inside a gardener's greenhouse during part of a day.

5. What is the temperature at 11:00 am?   Answer: _____ °C

6. What is the lowest temperature recorded?   Answer: _____ °C

7. Between which two times does the temperature rise the most?
   Circle the correct answer.

   A 9:00 and 10:00   C 11:00 and 12:00   E 1:00 and 2:00
   B 10:00 and 11:00   D 12:00 and 1:00

/ 3

8. Frankie asked 19 people whether they prefer tea, coffee or hot chocolate. His results are shown in this pictogram.

    How many people said they prefer tea?

    Answer: _____

    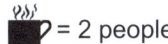 = 2 people

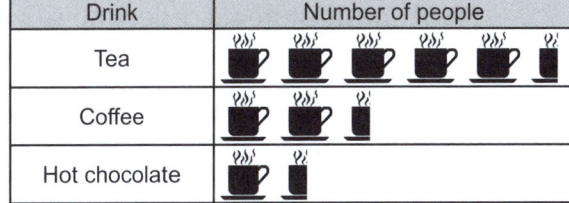

9. A group of tourists were asked in a survey to name their favourite English city. This bar chart shows the results.

    How many people took part in the survey?
    Circle the correct number.

    A 84   C 102   E 120
    B 92   D 110

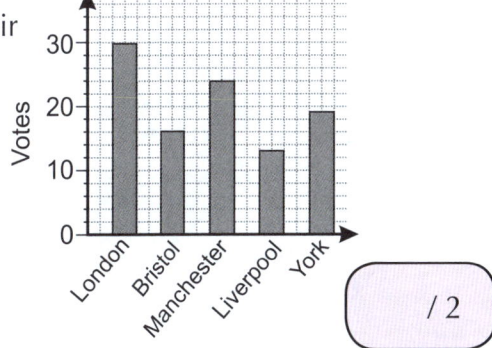

/ 2

Section Four — Data Handling

Displaying Data

10. This line graph shows how the height of a building changes as the number of floors it has increases.

    Using the graph, work out how tall a block of flats with 14 floors would be.

    Answer: _____ m

    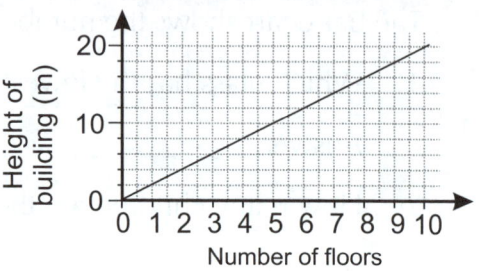

11. This dual bar chart shows the number of hours Sam and Sanjay worked out at the Fitness Centre over a three-week period.

    Over the three weeks, how many more hours did Sam spend working out than Sanjay?

    Answer: _____ hours

    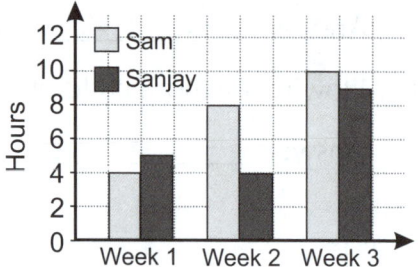

12. The pie charts below show the results of two schools in a rugby tournament. Each school played 32 matches. Which of these statements is true? Circle the correct answer.

    A Both sides won the same number of matches.
    B Eastwick School played sixteen drawn matches.
    C Southport School was undefeated fifteen times.
    D Southport School had the more successful side.
    E Both sides won a total of eighteen games.

    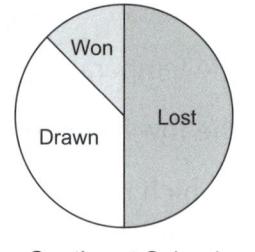

    Southport School 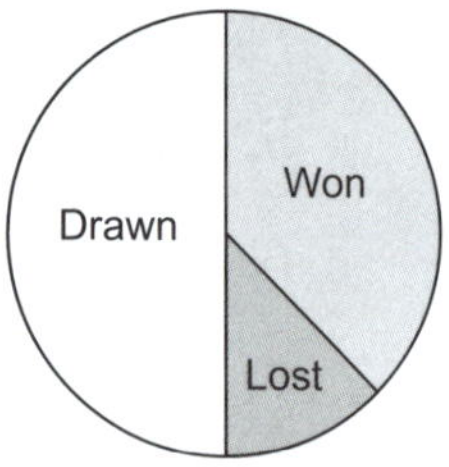   Eastwick School

13. A music store recorded the CD sales of three bands in this pictogram.

    How many more CDs did the Victories sell than the Moofs?

    Answer: _____

    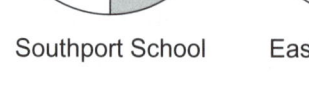 = 4 CDs

    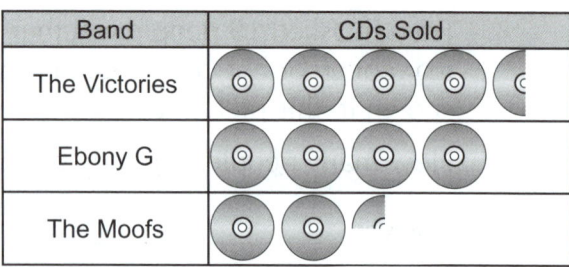

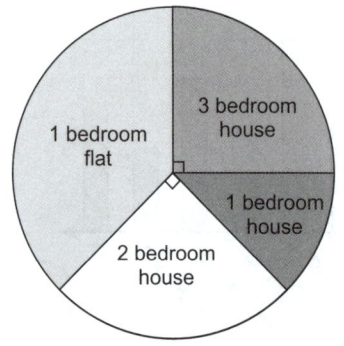

14. This pie chart shows the types of homes 80 people live in.

    How many people live in houses with more than 1 bedroom?

    Answer: _____

    /5

Section Four — Data Handling

The Mean

Work out the mean of the following sets of numbers.

1. 4, 3, 7, 8, 8   Answer: _____

2. 8, 12, 8, 7, 10   Answer: _____

3. 5, 9, 7, 6, 4, 17   Answer: _____

4. 9, 8, 10, 12, 9, 12   Answer: _____

5. 10, 8, 11, 11, 2, 4, 12, 6   Answer: _____

/ 5

6. Rajeev sprints for 80 m five times. The times taken to sprint each 80 m are shown below.

         14 s   12 s   15 s   17 s   12 s

What is his mean time?   Answer: _____ s

7. In a cricket match, the players in Jo's team scored the following numbers of runs.

     2   3   9   10   12   3   5   7   19   20   31

What is the mean score?   Answer: _____

8. The amount of rainfall measured in Showerham on four separate days is shown below.

         9 mm   12 mm   14 mm   13 mm

What is the mean rainfall?   Answer: _____ mm

/ 3

9. Katie and Vikram are competing in a darts competition. Their scores after 3 darts are written on the scoreboard.

What is the mean score with the six darts?

Answer: _____

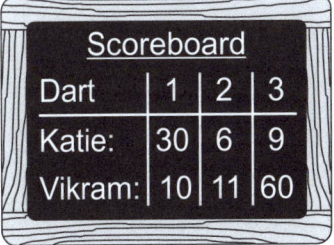

Scoreboard			
Dart	1	2	3
Katie:	30	6	9
Vikram:	10	11	60

10. Which of these groups of five numbers has a mean of 10?
    Circle the correct answer.

    A   12, 14, 13, 11, 12   C   8, 27, 19, 17, 4   E   16, 4, 9, 7, 14

    B   32, 20, 24, 29, 34   D   13, 9, 11, 5, 17

/ 2

Section Four — Data Handling

Section Five — Shape and Space

Angles

Use the angles marked in the shape on the right to answer these questions.

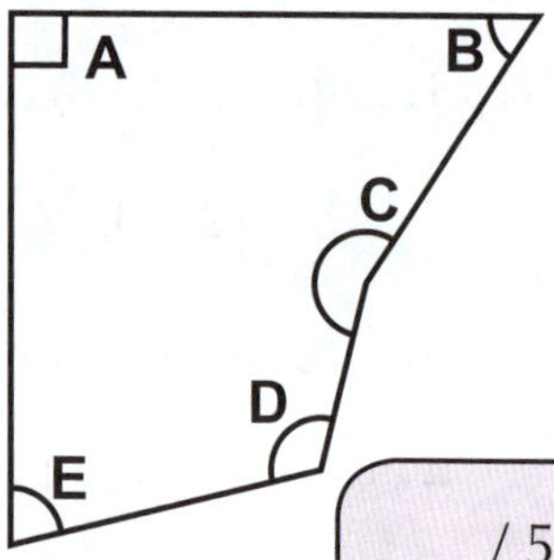

1. Which angle is a right angle? Answer: _____
2. Which angle is biggest? Answer: _____
3. Which two angles are acute angles? Answer: _____ and _____
4. Which angle is an obtuse angle? Answer: _____
5. Which angle is a reflex angle? Answer: _____

/ 5

Look at these angles.

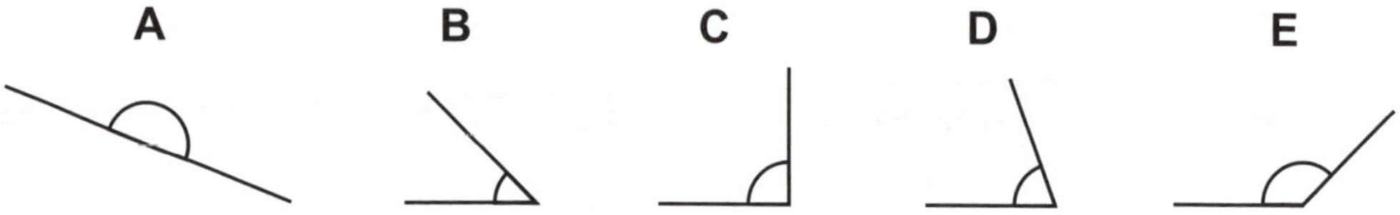

A   B   C   D   E

6. Which angle is most likely to be 45°? Answer: _____
7. Which angle is 180°? Answer: _____
8. Which angle is most likely to be 135°? Answer: _____
9. Which angle is most likely to be 70°? Answer: _____
10. Which angle is most likely to be 90°? Answer: _____

/ 5

11. An ant crawls the route shown below. How many times does the ant turn through a right angle? Circle the correct answer.

    0   1   2   3   4

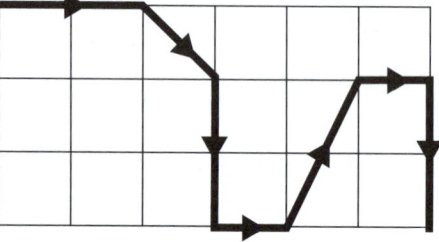

12. Paul is facing north. He turns clockwise to face west. What angle does he turn through?

Answer: _____°

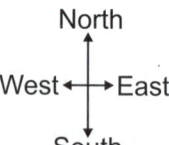

13. What is the size of angle x between the minute hand and the hour hand at four o'clock? Circle the correct answer.

    90°   120°   240°   180°   150°

14. Calculate angle y. Answer: _____°

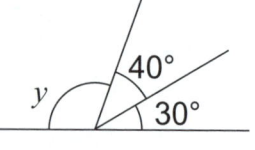

/ 4

Section Five — Shape and Space

2D Shapes

Write down the letter of the shape which matches each description.

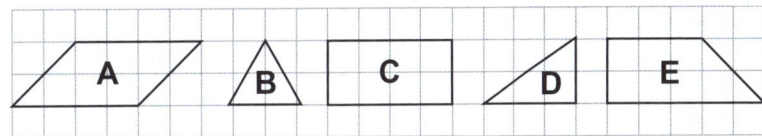

1. Three sides and no right angles.   Answer: _____
2. Four right angles.   Answer: _____
3. Exactly one right angle.   Answer: _____
4. Two pairs of parallel sides and no right angles.   Answer: _____
5. Exactly one obtuse angle.   Answer: _____

/ 5

Look at the lines on the right.
Decide whether each statement is true or false.

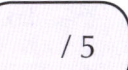

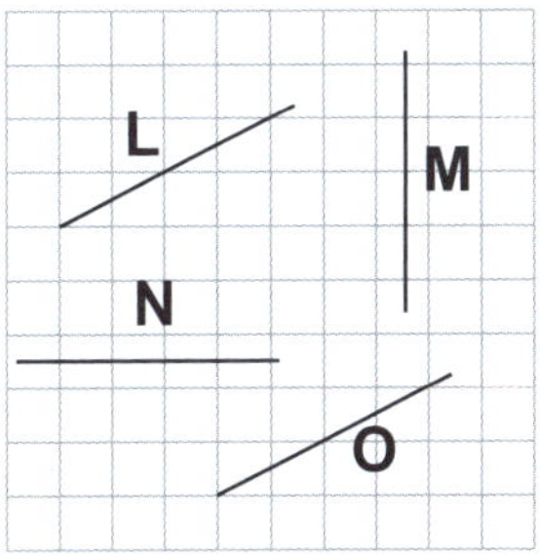

6. Line L is parallel to Line M.   Answer: _____
7. Line N is a horizontal line.   Answer: _____
8. Line L is a vertical line.   Answer: _____
9. Line L is parallel to Line O.   Answer: _____
10. Line M is perpendicular to Line N.   Answer: _____

/ 5

11. What is the name of the shape on the right? Circle the correct answer.

    triangle   octagon   pentagon   hexagon   quadrilateral

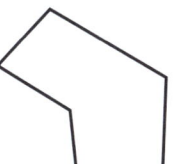

12. Which shape below should go in the shaded part of this diagram? Circle the correct answer.

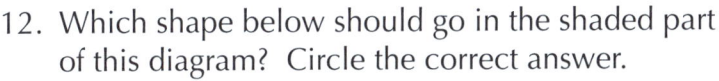

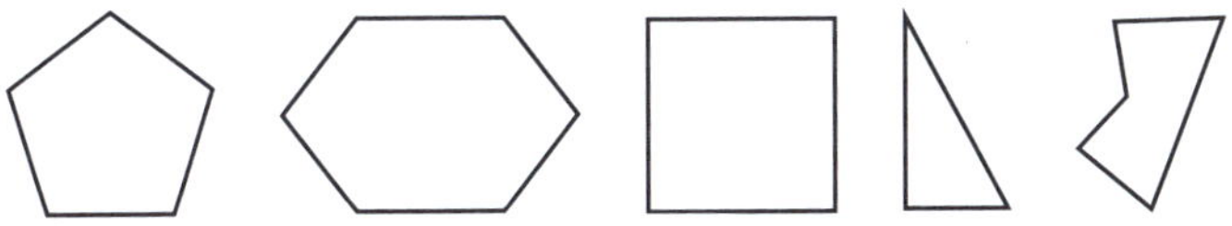

A   B   C   D   E

	Less than five sides	Five or more sides
Regular		
Irregular	▓	

13. Caley cuts six shapes out of a piece of paper and arranges them to make this picture. Which shapes did she use? Circle the correct answer.

    A 3 pentagons, 2 octagons, 1 rectangle
    B 3 hexagons, 2 octagons, 1 quadrilateral
    C 3 pentagons, 2 octagons, 1 quadrilateral
    D 2 pentagons, 3 octagons, 1 quadrilateral
    E 3 pentagons, 2 octagons, 1 parallelogram

/ 3

Section Five — Shape and Space

2D Shapes

14. Which of these shapes cannot fit together with other shapes of the same kind without leaving any gaps? Circle the correct answer.

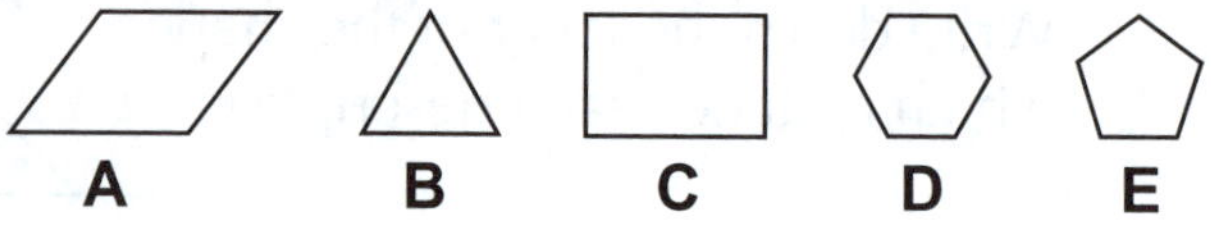

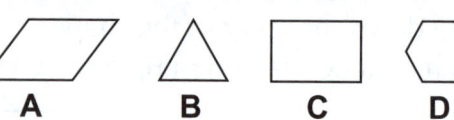

15. Molly is describing a shape. She says, "It has three sides. Only two of the angles are equal.". What shape is she describing? Circle the correct answer.

    equilateral triangle   hexagon   pentagon   quadrilateral   isosceles triangle

16. Maryam has a shape. Part of the sorting diagram she uses to identify it is shown on the right. Maryam answers 'Yes' to the first two questions. Which of the shapes below could she have? Circle the correct answer.

    triangle   parallelogram
    kite   hexagon
    pentagon

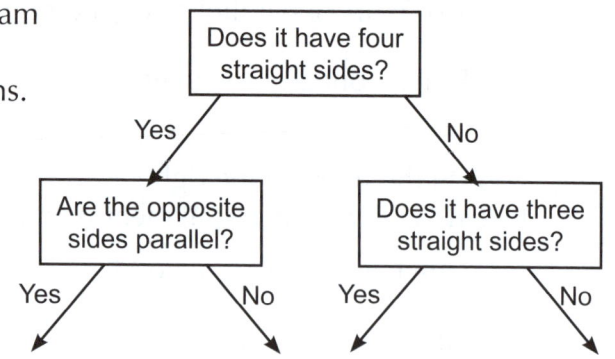

17. Work out the name of this quadrilateral from these clues:
    1. It has two pairs of equal length sides.
    2. No sides are parallel.
    3. The diagonals cross at right angles.   Answer: _____

18. Which of these statements about triangles is true? Circle the correct answer.

    A A triangle can have two right angles
    B An equilateral triangle has three acute angles.
    C A scalene triangle must have an obtuse angle.
    D The angles in a triangle always add up to 200 degrees.
    E An isosceles triangle has three equal sides.

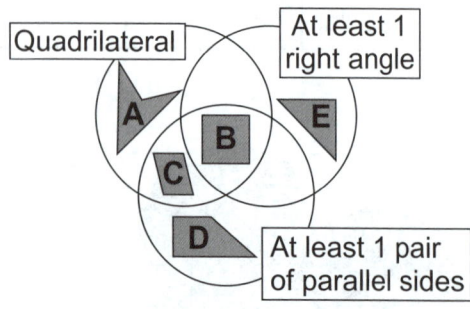

19. Look at this Venn diagram.
    Which shape is in the wrong place?

    Answer: _____

20. The sizes of three of the angles in this kite are given. What size is angle p?

    Answer: _____°

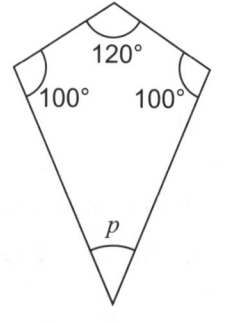

/7

2D Shapes — Perimeter and Area

Kate drew four shapes onto squared paper. Each square on the paper has sides of 1 cm.

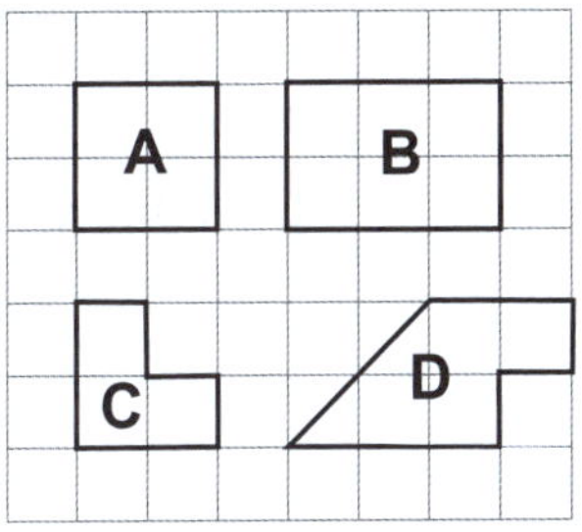

1. What is the perimeter of shape A? Answer: _____ cm

2. What is the area of shape B? Answer: _____ cm^2

3. What is the area of shape C? Answer: _____ cm^2

4. What is the area of shape D? Answer: _____ cm^2

5. What is the perimeter of shape C? Answer: _____ cm

/ 5

The dimensions of three shapes are shown on the right.

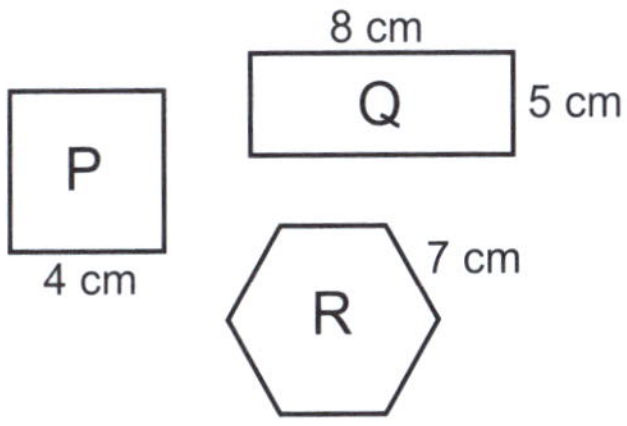

The diagrams on this page are not drawn to scale.

6. What is the perimeter of square P? Answer: _____ cm

7. What is the perimeter of rectangle Q? Answer: _____ cm

8. What is the area of square P? Answer: _____ cm^2

9. What is the area of rectangle Q? Answer: _____ cm^2

10. Shape R is a regular polygon. What is its perimeter? Answer: _____ cm

/ 5

11. These five letters are drawn on a 1 cm^2 grid. Which of these letters does not have an area of 7 cm^2? Circle the correct answer.

    A   B   C   D   E

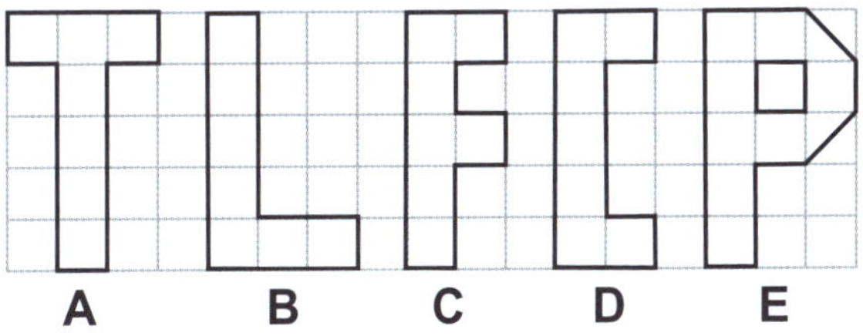

12. Which two of these shapes have the same area?

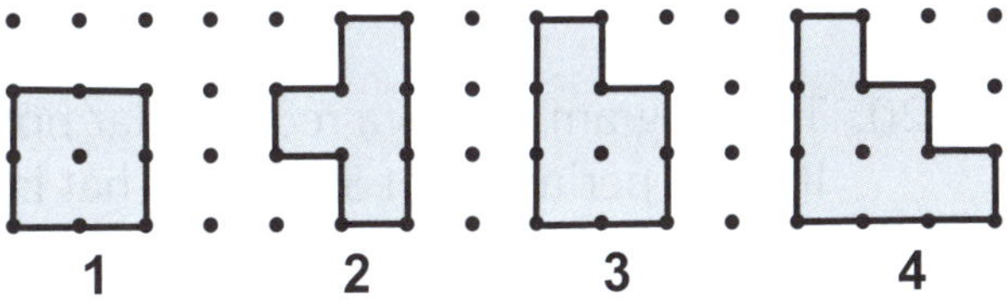

    Answer: _____ and _____

13. What units would be most suitable to use to measure the area of a tennis court? Circle the correct answer.

    m   m^2 cm^2 km^2 mm^2

14. Carlos has some table mats in the shape of regular octagons. The edges of the table mats are each 20 cm long. Carlos puts 6 of the table mats together to make this shape. What is the perimeter of the hole in the middle of the shape?

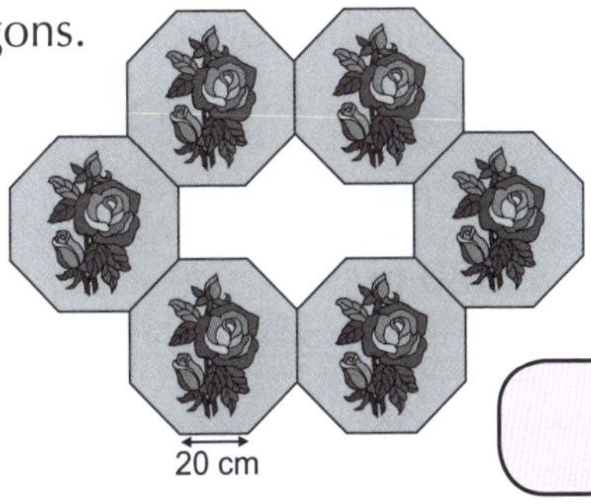

    Answer: _____ cm

/ 4

Section Five — Shape and Space

2D Shapes — Perimeter and Area

15. What is the approximate area of the island shown on this map? Each square shows an area of 1 km². Circle the correct answer.

    A 6 km²   C 14 km²   E 8 km²
    B 10 km²   D 12 km²

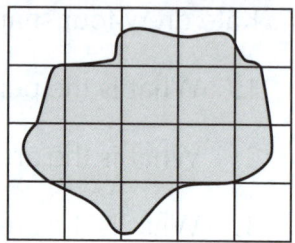

16. A rectangular swimming pool has an area of 72 m². Its width is 6 m. What is its length?

    Answer: _____ m

17. What is the area of the shape on the right?

    Answer: _____ cm²

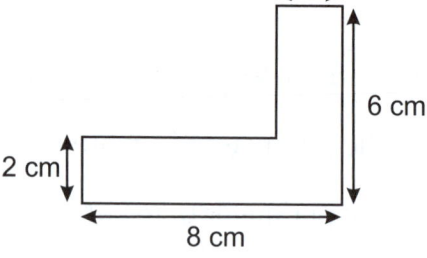

18. Mr Jones had a rectangular lawn measuring 15 m by 40 m. He built a square garage measuring 10 m by 10 m in the corner of his lawn. What area of lawn does he have left?

    Answer: _____ m²

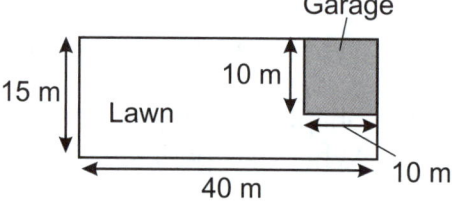

19. Ben is painting this cube. Its sides are 4 cm long. What is the total area that he paints?

    Answer: _____ cm²

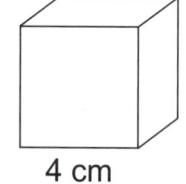 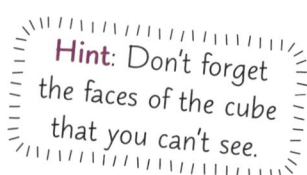

Hint: Don't forget the faces of the cube that you can't see.

20. The diagram shows a rectangular notepad. It has a perimeter of 50 cm. What is its width?

    Answer: _____ cm

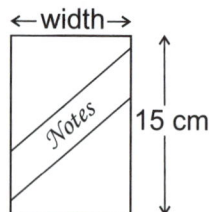

21. Here is a plan of Abdul's garden. He walks his dog around the edge of the garden ten times. How much less than one kilometre does he walk? Circle the correct answer.

    38 m   320 m
    62 m   620 m
    380 m

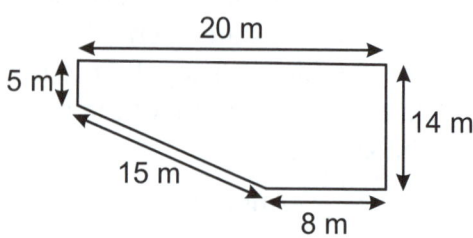

/7

Symmetry

Look at the letters on the right and answer questions 1-3.

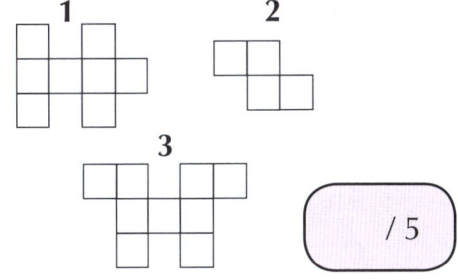

1. Which two of these letters have exactly one line of symmetry?   Answer: _____ and _____

2. Which of these letters has two lines of symmetry?   Answer: _____

3. Which two of these letters have no lines of symmetry?   Answer: _____ and _____

Use the shapes on the right to answer questions 4-5.

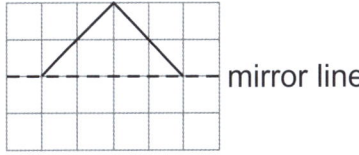

4. Which shape has a vertical line of symmetry?   Answer: _____

5. Which shape has a horizontal line of symmetry?   Answer: _____

/ 5

6. Which shape is made when the two lines are reflected in the mirror line? Circle the correct answer.

   square   parallelogram   triangle   pentagon   kite

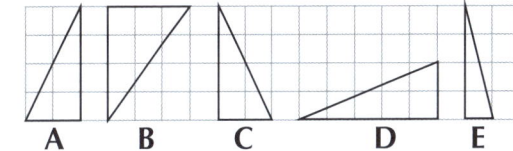

7. Which of these shapes is a reflection of shape P? Circle the correct answer.

8. Write down the number of the square that needs to be shaded to make a symmetrical pattern about the dashed mirror line.

   Answer: _____

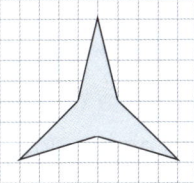

9. How many lines of symmetry does this shape have?

   Answer: _____

10. The patterned rectangle below is reflected in the mirror line. Which diagram shows the reflected rectangle? Circle the correct answer.

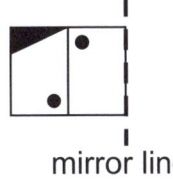
mirror line

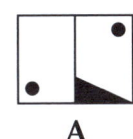
A

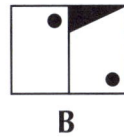
B

C

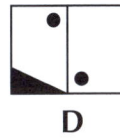
D

E

/ 5

Section Five — Shape and Space

3D Shapes

Look at these 3D shapes. Write the letter for each shape in the correct place in the table.

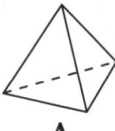 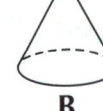 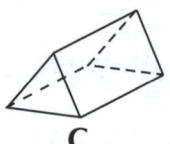 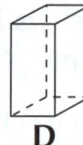 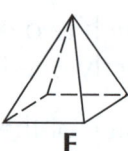

A   B   C   D   E

	Shape	Number of square or rectangular faces	Number of triangular faces	Number of circular faces
1.		3	2	0
2.		0	0	1
3.		6	0	0
4.		1	4	0
5.		0	4	0

/ 5

Answer questions 6-10 using shapes A-E above.

6. Which shape has 5 vertices?   Answer: _____

7. Which shape has 12 edges?   Answer: _____

8. Which shape has one edge and one vertex?   Answer: _____

9. Which two shapes are pyramids?   Answer: _____ and _____

10. Which two shapes are prisms?   Answer: _____ and _____

/ 5

11. What is the name of this 3D shape?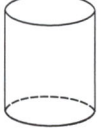

    Answer: _____

12. Which two of these shapes are nets of closed cubes?

    Answer: _____ and _____

    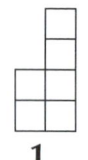 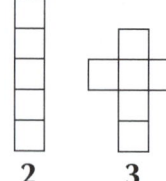 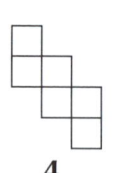 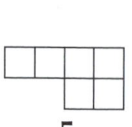

    1   2   3   4   5

13. Which of the following statements is false?

    A A cylinder has a curved face.
    B A cube has eight vertices.
    C A cone is a type of triangular prism.
    D Half a sphere is called a hemisphere.
    E All the angles in a cuboid are right-angles.

14. This cuboid is made of 1 cm³ blocks. What is its volume?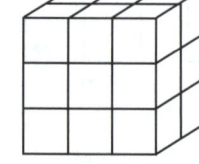

    Answer: _____ cm³

/ 4

Section Five — Shape and Space

3D Shapes

15. Which of the shapes below should go in the shaded box in this sorting diagram? Circle the correct answer.

    A cylinder
    B cone
    C triangular prism
    D sphere
    E cuboid

    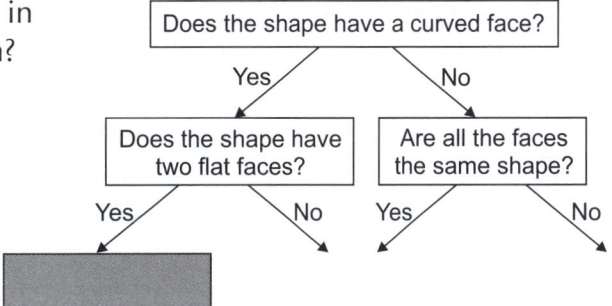

16. How many one centimetre cubes will fit into the cardboard box on the right?

    Answer: _____

    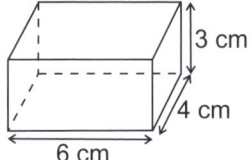

17. What 3D shape can be constructed from this net? Circle the correct answer.

    A cone   C triangular-based pyramid   E triangular prism
    B cube   D square-based pyramid

    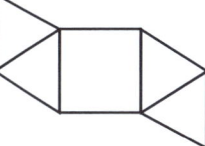

18. The opposite faces of a dice add up to seven. What number should replace X on this net of a dice?

    Answer: _____

    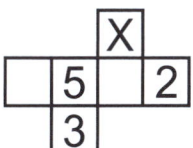

19. Look at this cuboid. One edge is marked by an X. How many edges are parallel to this edge? Circle the correct answer.

    1   2   3   5   7

    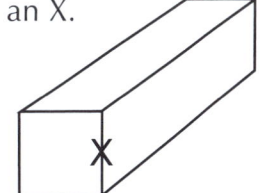

    Hint: You can't see all of the edges on this diagram of a cuboid.

20. The cube on the right has shaded triangles on three faces. Which of the following is the net of this cube? Circle the correct answer.

    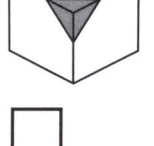

    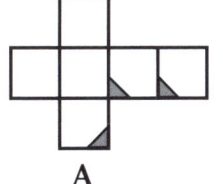   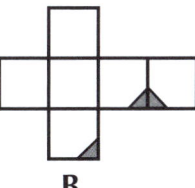   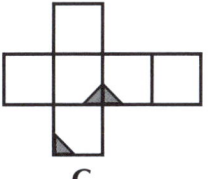   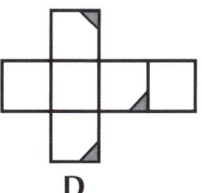   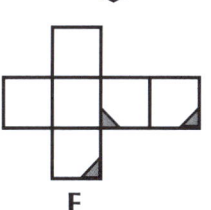
       A   B   C   D   E

21. A cuboid is 4 cm long and 2 cm wide. If it has a volume of 88 cm^3, what is its height?   Answer: _____ cm

/ 7

Section Five — Shape and Space

Shape Problems

Look at this piece of card with five holes in it.
Gilbert has a card shape, which is labelled P, below.

Which hole will shape P fit into if:

1. Gilbert rotates the shape 90° clockwise?   Answer: _____

2. Gilbert rotates the shape 90° anti-clockwise?   Answer: _____

3. Gilbert turns the shape over and rotates it?   Answer: _____

4. Which hole has a line of symmetry?   Answer: _____

5. Which two of the shapes below fit together to make shape P?

      Answer: _____ and _____   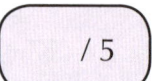   / 5

6. Here is a cube with an open top and the net from which it is made. Write down the number of the face that will form the base of the box.

   Answer: _____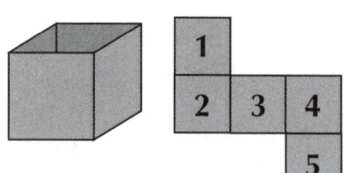

7. Here are six quadrilaterals. Which two are exactly the same shape?

   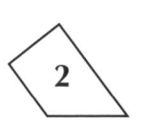 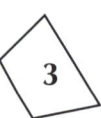

   Answer: _____ and _____

8. Ann makes shape X from four cubes. Two circles are drawn on the shape. Which of the options below could be shape X in a different position? Circle the correct answer.

   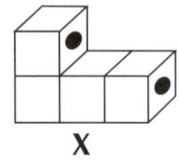 A 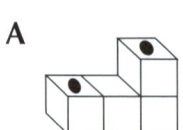 B 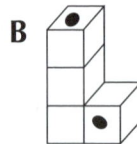 C 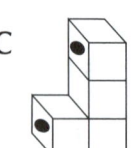 D 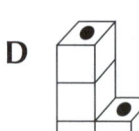 E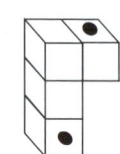

9. Shape F can be divided into four shapes that are identical to each other. Which of A–E is one of these shapes? Circle the correct answer.

   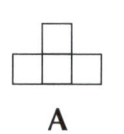 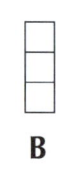 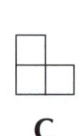 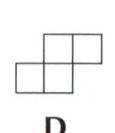    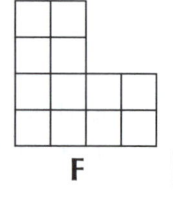

   A   B   C   D   E   F   / 4

Section Five — Shape and Space

Coordinates

Write the coordinates of the centre of each of these shapes.

1. Shape A   Answer: (_____ , _____)
2. Shape B   Answer: (_____ , _____)
3. Shape C   Answer: (_____ , _____)
4. Shape D   Answer: (_____ , _____)
5. Shape E   Answer: (_____ , _____)

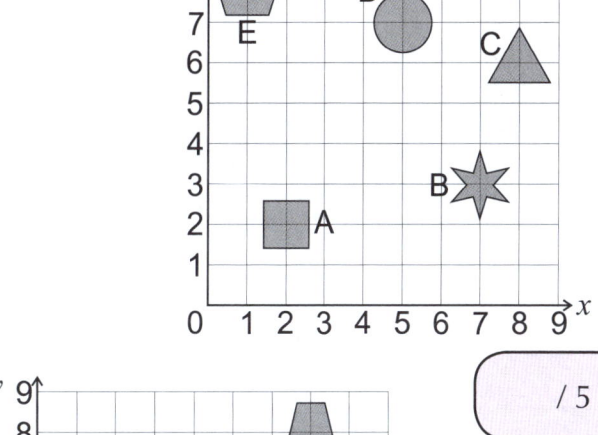

/ 5

Write the letter of the shape which has its centre at each of these points.

6. (1, 1)   Answer: _____
7. (7, 8)   Answer: _____
8. (8, 2)   Answer: _____
9. (4, 4)   Answer: _____
10. (2, 6)   Answer: _____

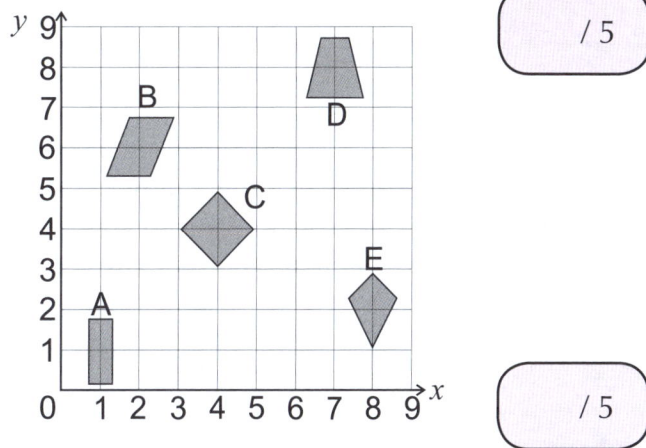

/ 5

11. Jack starts at the tree shown on the map.
    He moves 2 squares west and then 1 square south.
    What are the coordinates of the point he finishes at?

    Answer: (_____ , _____)

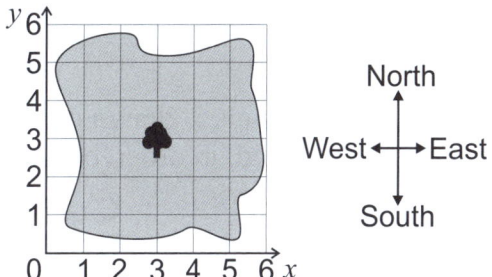

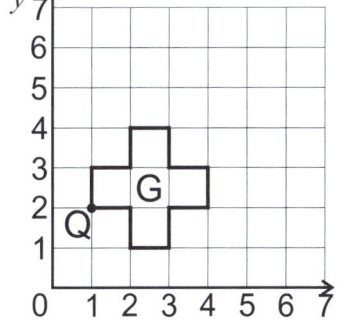

12. Shape G on the grid is translated 3 squares right and 5 squares up to give shape H. What will the new coordinates of point Q be?

    Answer: (_____ , _____)

13. The shape shown on the grid is reflected in the mirror line.
    What are the new coordinates of point A?
    Circle the correct answer.

    (6, 3)   (6, 2)   (6, 4)   (2, 6)   (5, 3)

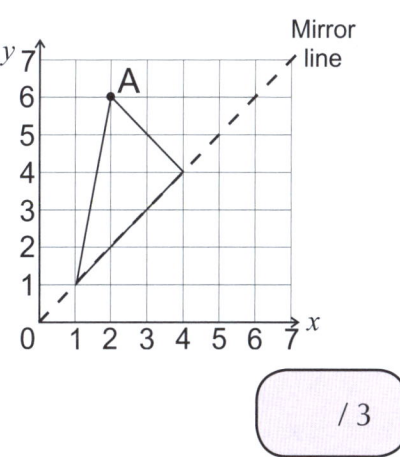

/ 3

Section Five — Shape and Space

Coordinates

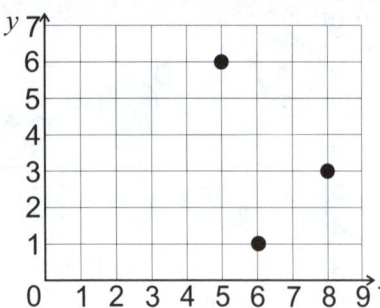

14. Three corners of a rectangle are marked on this grid. What are the coordinates of the rectangle's fourth corner?

    Answer: (_____, _____)

15. Find the coordinates of the midpoint of this line.

    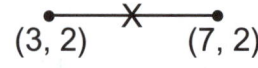

    Answer: (_____, _____)

16. Three corners of a kite are marked on this grid. What could be the coordinates of the kite's fourth corner? Circle the correct answer.

    A (4, 3)   D (3, 6)
    B (5, 0)   E (5, 2)
    C (2, 5)

    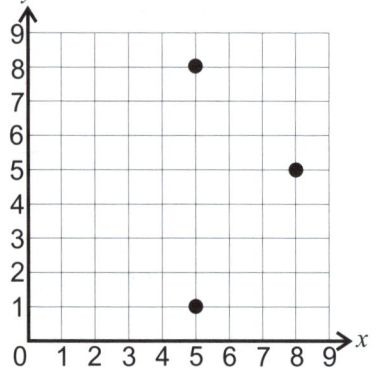

17. What shape is drawn if the points (0, 0), (1, 2), (3, 2) and (2, 0) are joined, in order, by straight lines? Circle the correct answer.

    A square   C parallelogram   E trapezium
    B rectangle   D pentagon

    Hint: If you can't picture what the shape looks like, try sketching the points on a rough piece of paper.

18. The coordinates of three corners of a rectangle are shown. What are the coordinates of corner A?

    A (2, 1)   D (4, 4)
    B (2, 4)   E (1, 2)
    C (1, 4)

    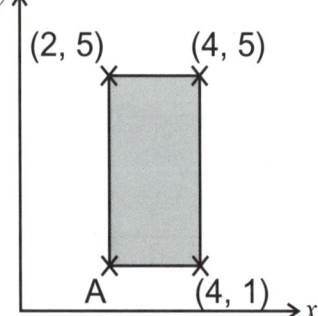

19. All three points on the diagram are the same distance apart. What are the coordinates of point P?

    Answer: (_____, _____)

    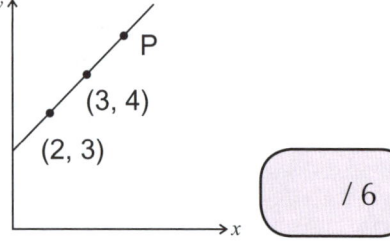

Section Five — Shape and Space

Section Six — Units and Measures

Units

| km | kg | l | ml | m | g |

Choose the most likely unit from those above to complete these sentences.

1. Kerry weighs 60 ...?... . Answer: _____

2. A giraffe is about 4.95 ...?... tall. Answer: _____

3. A bucket can hold about 18 ...?... of water. Answer: _____

4. A cake contains 125 ...?... of sugar. Answer: _____

5. Mount Everest is about 8.8 ...?... high. Answer: _____   / 5

6. Eve runs a race that is 5 km long. How far did she run in metres? Answer: _____ m

7. David has cycled 900 m. How much further does he need to go to reach one km? Answer: _____ m

8. How many millimetres are there in 7.9 cm? Answer: _____ mm

9. A bottle holds 0.5 l of orange juice. How many millilitres is this? Answer: _____ ml

10. James buys some bags of sweets. Each bag weighs 25 g. How many bags will he need to buy to have 1 kg of sweets? Answer: _____   / 5

11. Which of these is the most likely mass of an apple? Circle the correct answer.

    A 1000 g   **B** 150 g   **C** 5 g   **D** 1 g   **E** 10 g

12. What weight is shown on the set of scales? Give your answer in grams.

    Answer: _____ g

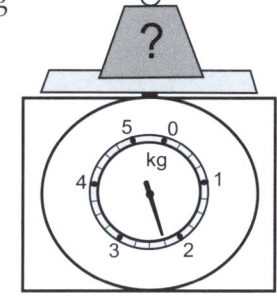

13. Which of the following statements is unlikely to be true? Circle the correct answer.

    A A walking route is 15 km long.

    B A dog measures 63 m from his nose to his tail.

    C A classroom is 9000 mm wide.

    D A door is 195 cm high.

    E An exercise book has a width of 180 mm.

Hint: Make sure you look at the units as well as the number when you're deciding if each option sounds sensible.

/ 3

Units

14. Zeke wants to measure the volume of milk he puts on his cereal. What would be the most sensible units to use?

    Answer: _____

15. Anita has a 0.5 kg bar of chocolate. If she eats 10 g of it, how many grams of chocolate does she have left?

    Answer: _____ g

16. A glass holds 250 ml. How many glassfuls could you pour from a 1½ litre bottle of lemonade?

    Answer: _____

17. Which of these is equal to 1500? Circle the correct answer.

    A The number of millilitres in 15 litres.
    B The number of millimetres in 150 centimetres.
    C The number of metres in 0.15 kilometres.
    D The number of grams in 150 kilograms.
    E The number of centimetres in 1.5 metres.

18. A plan has been drawn using the scale 1 cm = 50 cm. What would be the real length of a line drawn 8 cm long on the plan in metres?

    Answer: _____ m

19. Adam bakes a fruit cake that weighs 1 kg. He cuts away a section that weighs 50 g. Which diagram best shows the amount of cake that would be left? Circle the correct answer.

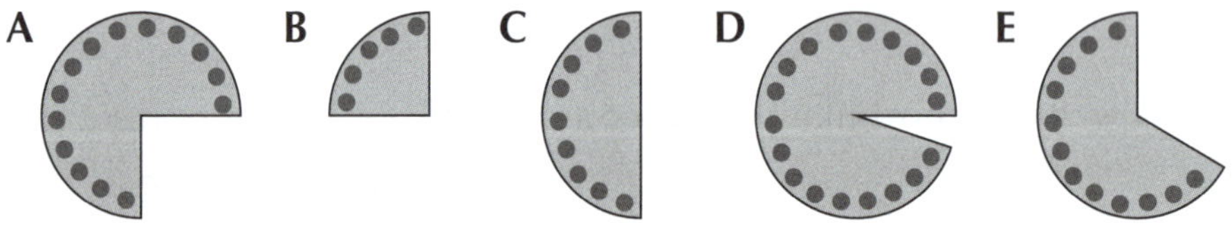

20. It takes 250 ml of paint to cover 1 m² of wall. Each tin holds 1 litre of paint. How many tins will be needed to paint a wall with a total area of 12 m²?

    Answer: _____

21. Matt has a piece of string that is 120 mm long. Kim has a piece of string that is 0.1 m long. How much longer is Matt's piece of string than Kim's piece of string in centimetres?

    Answer: _____ cm

22. A box containing 50 books weighs 15.5 kg. When the box is empty it weighs 500 g. How much does each book weigh?

    Answer: _____ g

/ 9

Time

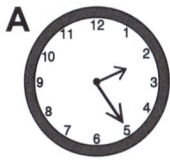 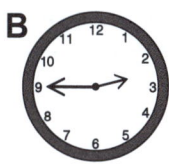  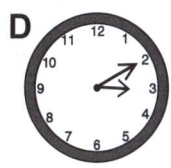

1. Kevin started travelling to his friend's house at the time shown on clock A. What time did Kevin set off? Answer: _____ : _____

2. Kevin was on the bus between the times shown on clocks B and C. How long was the bus journey? Answer: _____ minutes

3. Kevin got on a train at the time shown on clock D. The train journey was 45 minutes long. What time did he get off the train? Answer: _____ : _____

/ 3

The times shown below are all in the 24-hour clock.

| 20:25 | 05:25 | 17:25 | 15:25 | 12:15 |
| A | B | C | D | E |

4. Which clock shows a time in the morning? Answer: _____

5. Which clock shows the latest time in a day? Answer: _____

6. Which clock shows the time as 5:25 pm? Answer: _____

7. Which clock shows the time as twenty five past three? Answer: _____

8. What is the difference in the times shown by clocks E and D?

   Answer: _____ hours _____ minutes

/ 5

9. Circle the time below that is the same as 22:17.

   A 2:17 am   B 12:17 pm   C 10:17 am   D 10:17 pm   E 12:17 am

10. This is a train timetable for trains between Southwold and Westerton.

	Train A	Train B	Train C	Train D	Train E
Southwold	08:30	09:45	10:20	11:05	12:00
Eastford	08:45	10:10		11:30	
Northover	09:33	10:27	11:25	12:12	13:24
Westerton	10:00	11:15	12:11	12:47	13:58

What is the latest time that Sam could leave Southwold in order to be in time for an appointment in Northover at 12 noon? Answer: _____

11. How many days are there in total during March, April, May and June?

Answer: _____

/ 3

Section Six — Units and Measures

Time

12. Jane and Susan are identical twins. Jane was born at 8:15 am and Susan was born at 8:55 am. How many minutes older than Susan is Jane?

    Answer: _____ minutes

13. The table shows the start times of several television programmes. If you got home at 9:25 am, how long would you have to wait until the Cartoons started?

    Answer: _____ minutes

6:30	Breakfast Time
7:15	What's Happening
7:30	News
7:50	Learn with Ted
10:10	Cartoons

14. In 2011, January 9th was on a Sunday. What day of the week was January 26th in that year?   Answer: _____

15. A train was due to reach Preston at 4:25 am but it was one and three quarter hours late. What time did it arrive?   Answer: _____ am

16. Anita makes a New Year's resolution to eat an apple every day. If she starts on the 1st January, by what month will she have eaten 100 apples?   Answer: _____

17. When it is 14:10, what time was it thirty-five minutes ago?   Answer: _____

18. Sarah's birthday is on the 12th of June. On the 21st of May, how many days is it until Sarah's birthday?   Answer: _____

19. Johnny went to sleep at 10:15 pm. He woke up the next day at 7:30 am. How long did he sleep for?

    Answer: _____ hours _____ minutes

20. A film at the Astro Cinema starts at five to eight. It lasts for 1 hour 35 minutes. What time does the film finish?   Answer: _____

21. The table shows the times letters are collected from a post box. Anja posts a letter at 2:30 pm on Thursday. How long will it be before the letter is collected from the box?

    Answer: _____ hours _____ minutes

Monday to Friday	Saturday	Sunday
7 am 1 pm 2 pm	12:00 noon	No collection

22. These stopwatches show the times that Don and Ivor ran in a marathon. How much longer did Ivor take than Don?

    Answer: _____ minutes _____ seconds

    Don: 2 : 29 : 53   Ivor: 2 : 47 : 01

/ 11

Mixed Problems

1. Annie works from 9 am to 3 pm each day for 5 days. She is paid £210 in total. How much money does she earn each hour?

    Answer: £ _____

2. Suzy's test results are shown in the table. Her teacher added her three marks together and then rounded this to the nearest 10 to give her final mark. What was Suzy's final mark?

    Answer: _____

Subject	Mark
English	48
Maths	67
Science	50

3. It takes two builders 24 days to build one house. How many days would it take six builders to build two houses if they worked at the same speed? Circle the correct answer.

    A 8 days   **B** 24 days   **C** 12 days   **D** 18 days   **E** 16 days

4. A container holds 8 litres of water. A dripping tap adds 5 ml of water to the container every second. How many seconds will it take to half-fill the container?

    Answer: _____ s

5. Azhar drew three lines and reflected them in the mirror line to make a shape. What is the name of the shape? Circle the correct answer.

    A quadrilateral   **C** triangle   **E** hexagon

    B heptagon   **D** pentagon

6. Phil records the times he started and finished doing his homework over 3 days. What is the mean time Phil spends doing his homework each day?

    Answer: _____ minutes

Day	Start Time	Finish Time
Monday	4:15 pm	5:15 pm
Tuesday	5:05 pm	5:55 pm
Wednesday	5:30 pm	6:10 pm

7. The temperature in a greenhouse is 14 °C. A heater is switched on and the temperature in the greenhouse rises by 1 °C every 12 minutes. How long, in hours and minutes, will it take for the temperature in the greenhouse to reach 25°C?

    Answer: _____ hours and _____ minutes

8. A group of children take part in a 60-hour computer games challenge. If they start at 10:00 am on Friday, when will they finish? Circle the correct answer.

    A 10:00 pm on Sunday   **D** 10:00 am on Monday

    B 4:00 pm on Sunday   **E** 10:00 am on Sunday

    C 11:00 pm on Saturday

Mixed Problems

9. Four people go on a camping trip. They are charged 60p for each litre of water that they collect. Each person collects 2 litres of water every morning for the five days they are there. How much will they pay for the water altogether? Circle the correct answer.

   A £6   **B** £240   **C** £16   **D** £24   **E** £90

10. Which of the following is the correct formula for the perimeter of this isosceles triangle? Circle the correct answer.

    A $a \times b \times c$ **C** $2a + c$ **E** $2b + 2c$

    B $a \times b + c$ **D** $a + 2c$

    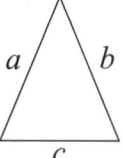

11. Carlo arranges 10 square chocolate brownies on a rectangular board as shown. Each brownie has 8 cm sides. He leaves a 4 cm border around the edge of the brownies. What is the length of the board that he uses?

    Answer: _____ cm

    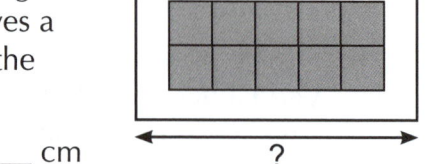

12. Each child pays £155 to go on a school trip to the Lake District. 20% of each child's payment is used to buy food. How much of each child's payment is not used to buy food?

    Answer: £ _____

13. Xavi is painting a rectangular wall. The wall is 4 metres long and 2.5 metres high. Xavi has painted 0.5 m² of the wall. What percentage of the wall has he painted?

    Answer: _____ %

14. Hanna throws a pair of dice six times. She records the numbers that she rolls in the table.

Throw	1	2	3	4	5	6
Numbers rolled	2 and 3	6 and 1	5 and 1	4 and 5	3 and 6	?

    Hanna adds the two numbers together to find her score for each throw. If her mean score is 7, what was her score in throw 6?

    Answer: _____

15. There are 32 children in Class 5S. The bar chart shows the number of children who have their birthday each month.

    The bar for March has not been drawn yet. What fraction of the class have their birthday in March? Circle the correct answer.

    1/6   1/8   4/16   2/5   1/4

    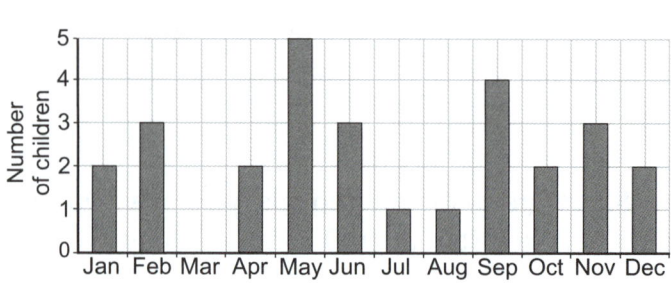

Section Seven — Mixed Problems

Assessment Test 1

The rest of the book contains five assessment tests to help you improve your maths skills. Allow 40 minutes to do each test and work as quickly and as carefully as you can.

If you want to attempt each test more than once, you will need to print **multiple-choice answer sheets** for these questions from our website — go to cgpbooks.co.uk/11plus/answer-sheets or scan the QR code on the right. If you'd prefer to answer them in standard write-in format, either write your answers in the spaces provided or circle the **correct answer** from the options **A to E**.

1. What is 1000 times 0.13?   Answer: _____

2. Which of these numbers is sixteen thousand and twenty six?

   A 1 600 026   **C** 16 260   **E** 16 026
   B 1626   **D** 1 600 206

3. Which of these numbers is the smallest?

   A 3.32   **B** 32   **C** 3.12   **D** 3.08   **E** 3.2

4. How many lines of symmetry does this rectangle have?

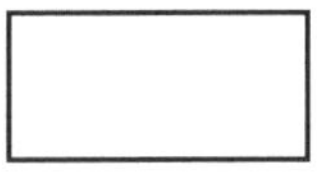

   Answer: _____

5. Chen wants to measure the length of a pencil.
   Which of these units would be the most sensible to use?

   A m   **B** km   **C** g   **D** cm   **E** ml

6. A rectangular floor tile measures 30 cm long and 15 cm across. What is the area of the tile?

   A 45 cm²   **C** 90 cm²   **E** 75 cm²
   B 450 cm²   **D** 4.5 m²

7. This chart shows the hair colours and hair lengths of children in Josie's school. How many children have long black or long brown hair?

   Answer: _____

	Short	Medium	Long
Blonde	44	0	21
Brown	64	15	43
Black	3	1	19
Other	17	0	0

8. What are the coordinates of the lighthouse on this map of an island?

   Answer: (_____ , _____)

9. Jamila has two hundred and one beads. She gives away 66. How many does she have left?

   Answer: _____

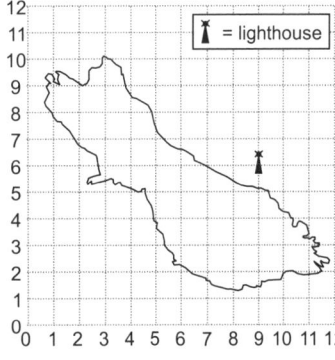

/ 9

Carry on to the next question → →

10. This shape is made by laying four isosceles triangles together, around a square. Each triangle is identical to triangle ABC.

    What is the perimeter of the shape?

    Answer: _____ cm

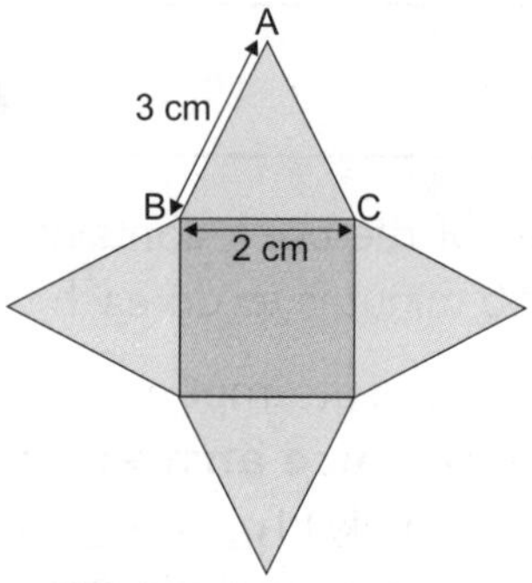

11. What is the weight of the grapes on the scale?

    A 1.53 kg   C 1.75 kg   E 1.7 kg
    B 1.65 kg   D 1.6 kg

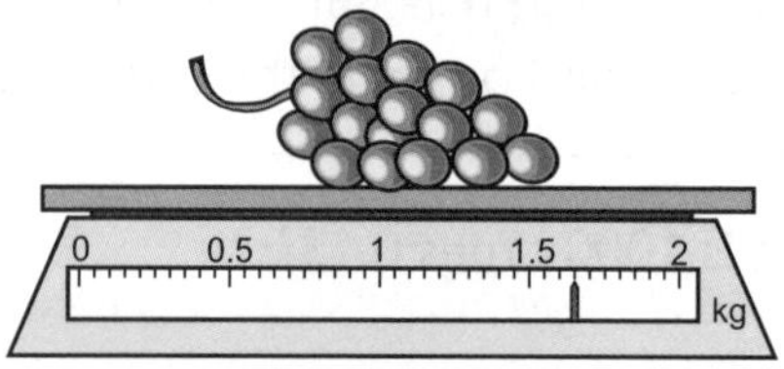

12. This pie chart shows how children travelled to school on one day. 70 children cycled to school.

    How many children walked to school?

    Answer: _____

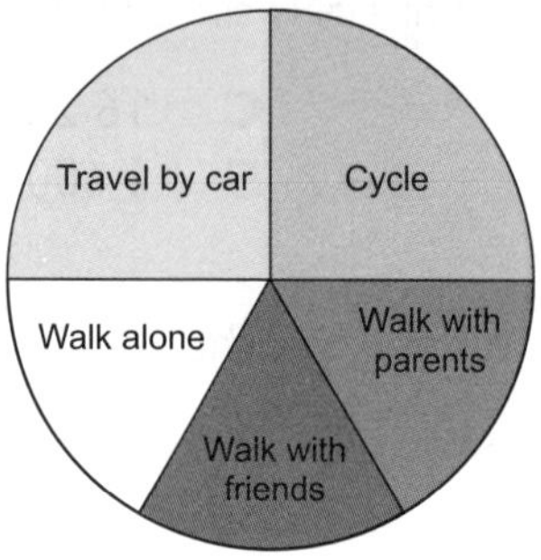

13. A shopping basket weighing 250 g contains 1.4 kg of beans and 2 apples weighing 160 g each. What is the total weight of the basket, beans and apples?

    A 1.81 kg   B 197 g   C 1810 g   D 1.97 kg   E 1.72 kg

14. A floor robot moves in the shape of an equilateral triangle.
    It turns to face the direction that it moves in.
    It finishes facing the same direction it started in.

    How many degrees has the robot turned through?   Answer: _____ °

15. How many 5p coins would be needed to make £3.35?   Answer: _____

16. Heike needs 300 tiles to tile a wall. The tiles come in packs of 50, which cost £6.50 each. What is the minimum amount Heike could spend to get the number of tiles he needs?

    Answer: £ _____

17. How many prime numbers are there between ten and thirty?   Answer: _____

Assessment Test 1

18. The pictogram shows the number of bicycles of each colour in the school bike shed.

    How many bicycles are there altogether?

    Answer: _____

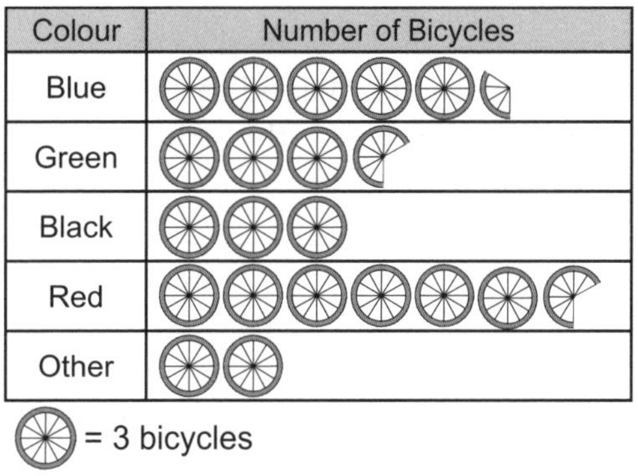

Colour	Number of Bicycles
Blue	5½ wheels
Green	3¼ wheels
Black	3 wheels
Red	7¼ wheels
Other	2 wheels

    ◉ = 3 bicycles

19. The lowest night time temperature was 26 °C colder than the highest daytime temperature of 18 °C.

    What was the coldest night time temperature?   Answer: _____ °C

20. Which of these numbers is not a multiple of 7?

    A 550   **B** 210   **C** 49   **D** 21   **E** 77

21. Chen has cut the first slice of this cake. All the other slices will be the same size.

    How many slices will there be altogether?

    Answer: _____

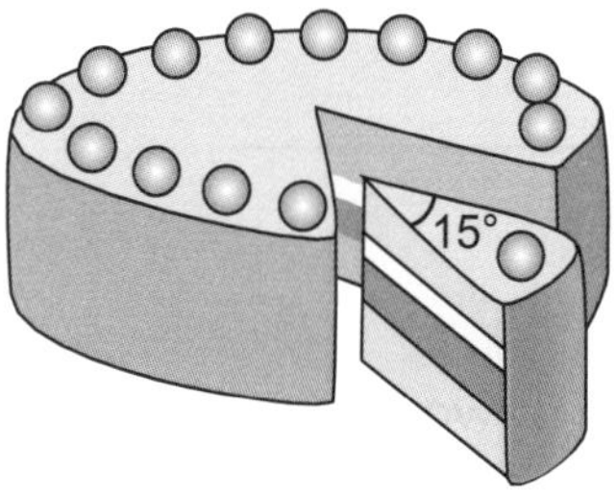

22. A disco started at the time shown on the clock. It finished when Alexa's digital watch showed 23:45.

    How long did the disco last?

    Answer: _____ hours _____ minutes

23. A biscuit weighs 25 g. 20% of each biscuit is fat. Charlie eats 3 biscuits. What weight of fat did Charlie eat?   Answer: _____ g

24. The triangle shown on the grid is reflected in the mirror line. What are the new coordinates of point C?

    Answer: (_____ , _____)

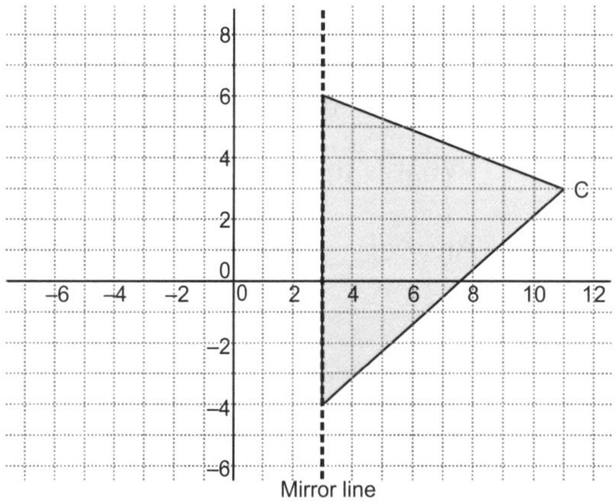

25. What is 6.9 × 3.1 rounded to the nearest whole number?

    A 25   **C** 12   **E** 21
    B 19   **D** 23

/ 8

Carry on to the next question → →

Assessment Test 1

26. What is the ratio of shaded to non-shaded sections in the shape on the right?

    Answer: _____ : _____

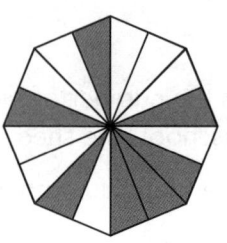

27. Every hour, Charles measures the amount of rain that has collected in a bucket in his back garden. His results for the first 8 hours are shown on the line graph.

    How much water was there in the bucket after 6 hours?

    Answer: _____ ml

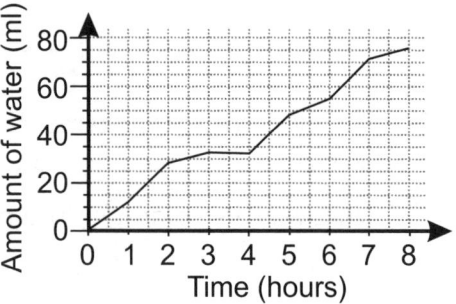

28. Josie builds this tower of blocks. She wants to continue the same pattern and add two more layers to the tower.

    How many more blocks will she need?

    Answer: _____

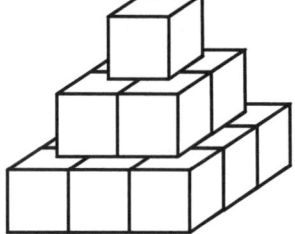

29. It takes 120 cm of wool to make a friendship bracelet. Two year 4 classes are making friendship bracelets. Each class has 25 children.

    How much wool will be needed for all year 4 children to make one bracelet each?

    Answer: _____ m

30. In a bag of assorted mints, 1 in every 8 are spearmint flavour. There are 104 mints in the bag, how many are spearmint flavour?

    Answer: _____

31. A class draws a bar chart showing the number of leaves on 21 pea plants they are growing.

    What is the most common number of leaves?

    Answer: _____

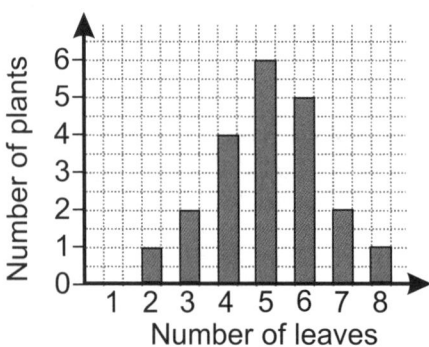

32. What is $\frac{3}{8}$ of 32?

    A 256 **B** 16 **C** 12 **D** 85 **E** 4

Assessment Test 1

33. The expression 2n + 1 can be used to find the numbers in a sequence. What is the 56th number in this sequence?   Answer: _____

34. A group of children drew a graph of the number of red cars that passed their school each hour.

    What was the mean number of red cars that passed the school each hour?

    Answer: _____

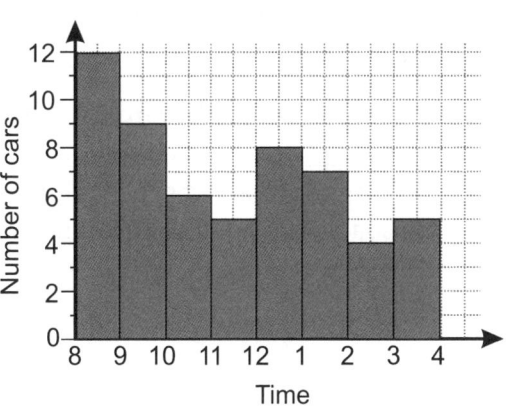

35. Richard gets paid £5.20 per hour for gardening and £4.80 per hour for cleaning.
    One day, Richard spent 3 hours gardening and 4 ½ hours cleaning.
    Which of these calculations gives the total amount Richard was paid?

    A £5.00 × 3 + 60p + 4 × £4.80 + £2.40
    B £5.00 × 3 − 60p + 4 × £4.80 − 2.40
    C £4.80 × 3 + 20p + 4.5 × £5.20
    D £4.80 × 4 − 20p + 5 × £5.20 − £2.60
    E £2.40 × 4 + £4.80 + 3 × £5.20

36. All the edges of a cube add to a total length of 48 cm.
    What is the area of one face of the cube?   Answer: _____ cm²

37. A rectangular yard is 0.2 m long and 7 m wide. What volume of concrete is needed to cover the yard with a concrete layer one tenth of a metre thick?

    A 104 m³   B 14 m³   C 1.4 m³   D 0.14 m³   E 0.014 m³

38. 64 × 1322 = 84 608   What is 32 × 1322?

    A 21 152   B 42 304   C 28 202   D 169 216   E 9562

39. A taxi fare costs a standing fee of £2 plus 30p per km.
    Which of these expressions gives the price of a journey of Y kms?

    A £2.30Y   B £23Y   C £2 + £0.3Y   D £2Y + £0.3   E £(2 + 3)Y

40. A school is preparing for a trip. One adult is needed to look after each group of six children.
    One coach has 42 seats. 162 children have paid for the trip.

    How many coaches will be needed?

    Answer: _____

/ 8

End of Test

Assessment Test 1

Assessment Test 2

Allow 40 minutes to do this test. Work as quickly and as carefully as you can.

You can print **multiple-choice answer sheets** for these questions from our website — go to cgpbooks.co.uk/11plus/answer-sheets or scan the QR code on the right. If you'd prefer to answer them in standard write-in format, either write your answers in the spaces provided or circle the **correct answer** from the options **A** to **E**.

1. Write fifty three thousand and twenty four in figures.   Answer: _____

2. Which three of these numbers add up to 100?   25   55   45   75   10   40   30
   A 25, 55, 30   **B** 55, 10, 30   **C** 45, 40, 10   **D** 45, 30, 25   **E** 75, 10, 25

3. Look at these shapes. What type of polygon are they?
   A pentagon   **C** quadrilateral   **E** heptagon
   B octagon   **D** hexagon

4. Which of these is the best estimate of the weight of a horse?
   A 40 g   **B** 40 kg   **C** 4 g   **D** 400 kg   **E** 400 g

5. Mark has a 180 g and a 90 g parcel to post.
   Use the information in the table to work out the minimum amount that Mark could pay to post his parcels.

Weight	Postage cost	
	1st Class	2nd Class
Up to 100 g	90p	69p
100 – 250 g	120p	110p
251 – 500 g	160p	140p
Over 500 g	230p	190p

   Answer: £ _____

6. What is the next number in this sequence?
   145   146   148   151   155   ?   Answer: _____

7. Which of these numbers can be placed into the shaded area of this Venn diagram?
   A 2
   B 3
   C 5
   D 7
   E 12

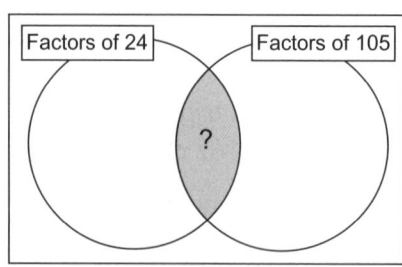

/ 7

8. The diagram shows the pattern of floor tiles in Andy's kitchen.
   What percentage of the floor tiles are shaded?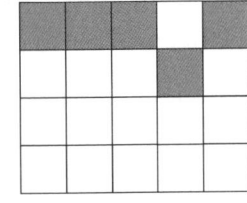

   A 20%   C 50%   E 5%
   B 30%   D 25%

9. $24 \times 4 = 96$ What is 24×400?   Answer: _____

10. Chunni measures the circumference of her bicycle wheel.
    Which of these is most likely to be the circumference of the wheel?

    A 1.70 cm   B 17 cm   C 17 m   D 17000 mm   E 1.7 m

11. Look at these models: 1 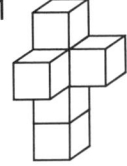 2 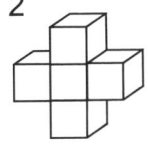 3 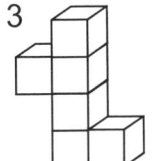 4 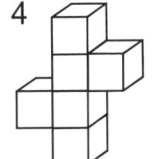 5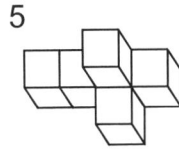

    Write down the numbers of the two models that are identical.

    Answer: _____ and _____

12. The times below are shown on a 24-hour digital clock.
    Which time is closest to midnight?

    | 00:35 | 01:02 | 22:55 | 23:35 | 00:55 |
    | A | B | C | D | E |

13. This tally chart and bar chart show the number of different types of flowers in a flower bed. The data for one type of flower has not been drawn on the bar chart.

Flower	Tally	Total
Daisies	ЖЖ ЖЖ ЖЖ ЖЖ ЖЖ ЖЖ	30
Buttercups	ЖЖ ЖЖ ЖЖ IIII	19
Dandelions	ЖЖ ЖЖ ЖЖ	15
Stitchwort	ЖЖ ЖЖ ЖЖ II	17
Chickweed	ЖЖ ЖЖ ЖЖ ЖЖ ЖЖ ЖЖ ЖЖ I	36

    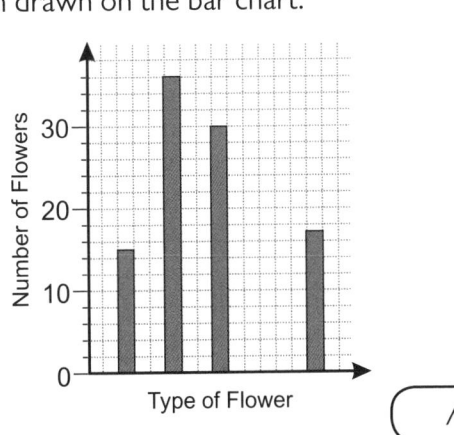

    Which type of flower is missing from the bar chart?

    Answer: _____

/ 6

Carry on to the next question → →

14. The pie chart shows how many children wear full uniform, part of the uniform or no uniform at a school.

    What fraction of the total number of children wear full school uniform?

    A ¼   B ½   C ¾   D ⅙   E ⅓

    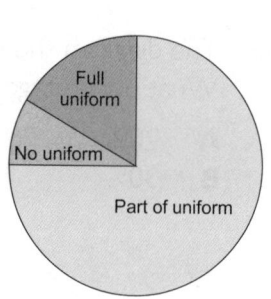

15. One Saturday, the temperature in Quebec was −16°C and the temperature in England was 5 °C. What was the temperature difference between Quebec and England?

    Answer: _____ °C

16. The rectangle on the right is drawn on a 1 cm square grid. What is the area of the shaded triangle?

    Answer: _____ cm²

    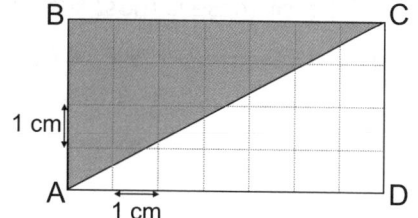

17. Which of these numbers is a multiple of 3?

    A 334   B 101   C 227   D 211   E 177

18. The table below shows the number of pictures on each page of a children's story book.

Number of pictures	1	2	3	4	5	6	7	8
Number of pages	5	9	6	14	9	21	9	11

    What is the most common number of pictures on a page?

    Answer: _____

19. What is $^{17}/_2$ as a decimal?

    A 9.8   C 17.5   E 9.2
    B 7.4   D 8.5

20. Which of the angles in this shape is closest to a right-angle?

    A   B   C   D   E

    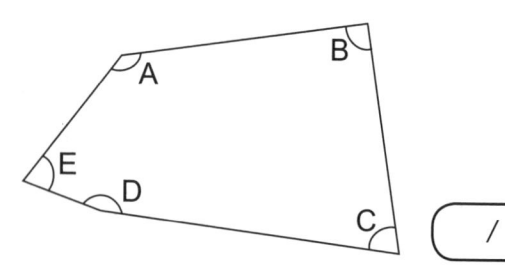

/ 7

Assessment Test 2

21. The number of hours of rain on each day was recorded for five days. The pictogram shows the result.

    How many more hours of rain were there on Monday than on Thursday?

    Answer: _____ hours

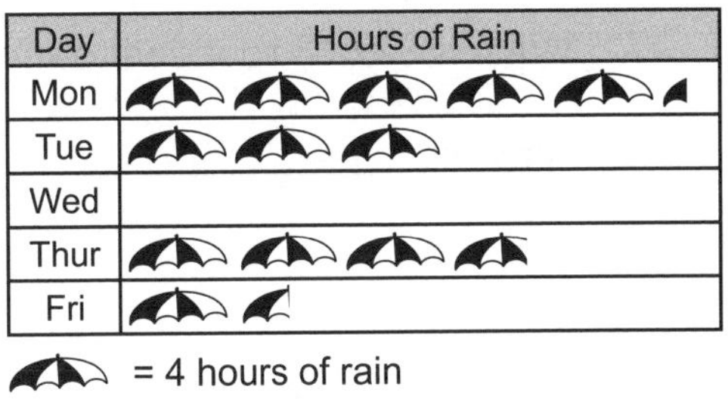

Day	Hours of Rain
Mon	☂ ☂ ☂ ☂ ☂◐
Tue	☂ ☂ ☂
Wed	
Thur	☂ ☂ ☂ ☂
Fri	☂ ◐

    ☂ = 4 hours of rain

22. One flapjack needs 20 g of sugar.
    Reiko has a 2 kg bag of sugar.

    How much sugar will she have left after she has made 25 flapjacks?

    Answer: _____ g

23. Niamh watches a film that was released in the year MCMXCIX.
    Niamh was born in 2007.

    How many years older than Niamh is the film?

    Answer: _____ years

24. Three corners of a parallelogram have been marked on this grid.
    What are the coordinates of the fourth corner?

    A (2, 3)   **C** (3, 2)   **E** (4, 2)
    B (2, 2)   **D** (1, 1)

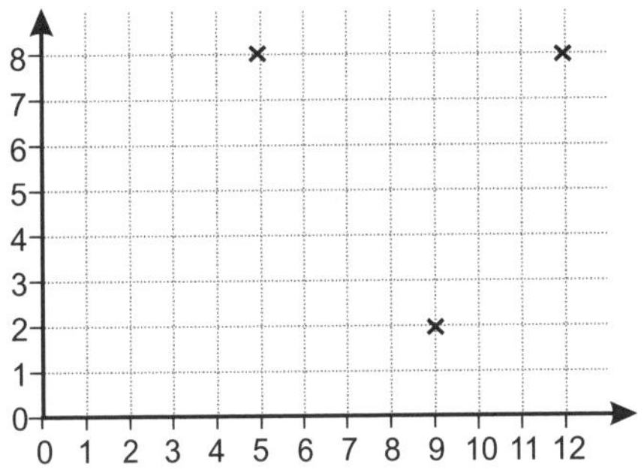

25. Sanji is selling ice creams and needs to buy thirty ice cream cones. He can buy normal cones or waffle cones.

    Waffle cone: 46p each
    Normal cone: 36p each

    How much more would it cost him to buy waffle cones instead of normal cones?

    Answer: £ _____

26. The net in the diagram on the right is folded to form a cube. Which face of the cube will the arrow point to?

    A   **B**   **C**   **D**   **E**

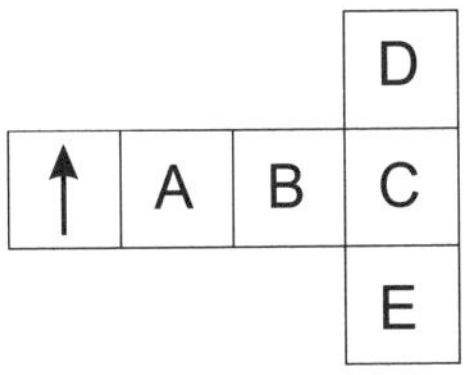

/ 6

Carry on to the next question → →

Assessment Test 2

27. What is 872.63 rounded to the nearest tenth?

    Answer: _____

28. 378 fish were divided equally between 9 fish tanks.
    How many fish were put in each tank?

    Answer: _____

29. This shape is made from four identical rectangles each measuring 8 cm by 2 cm. What is the perimeter of this shape?

    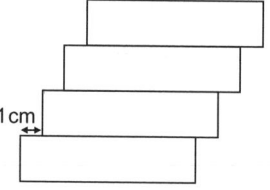

    Answer: _____ cm

30. A shop sells mugs in small packs of 4 for £5.50, or large packs of 12 for £15. Caleb buys one large pack and two small packs of mugs.

    What was the mean price he paid for a mug?   Answer: £ _____

31. This line graph shows how the temperature changed during one week.

    What was the difference between the highest temperature and the lowest temperature during the week?

    Answer: _____ °C

    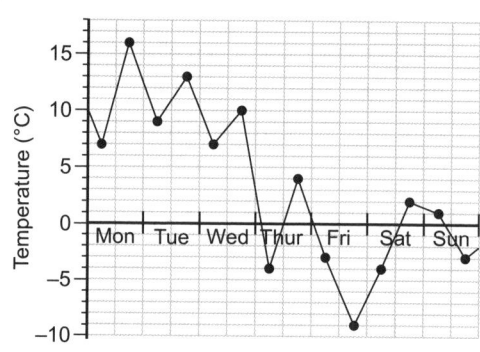

32. Sandy bought 6 postcards at 49p each and 5 postcards at 99p each.
    How much change did she receive from £10?

    Answer: £ _____

33. The instructions on the bottle of lemon squash are to dilute one measure of juice with five measures of water. Nico pours squash into the measuring jug, as shown in the diagram, and then adds the correct amount of water.

    How much squash does he make?

    A 0.6 litres   C 9 litres   E 600 litres
    B 0.9 litres   D 900 litres

    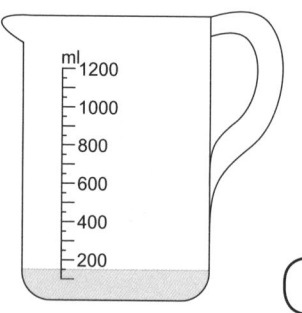

    / 7

34. A car can travel 8.5 miles per litre of fuel.
    How many miles can it travel on 40 litres of fuel?

    Answer: _____ miles

35. Look at this number line.
    Which of these statements is true?

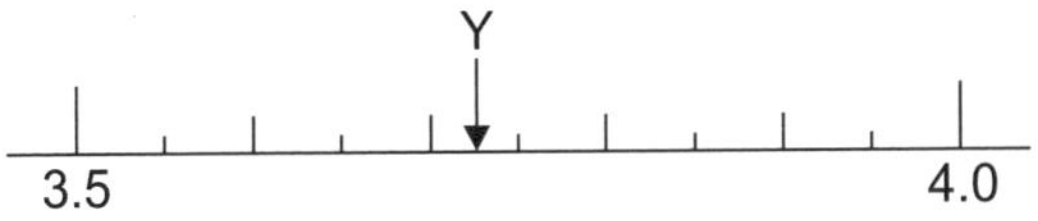

    A Y > 3.75   D Y < 3.65
    B Y > 3.8   E Y = 3.80
    C Y < 3.75

36. What is the size of angle *k*?

    Answer: _____ °

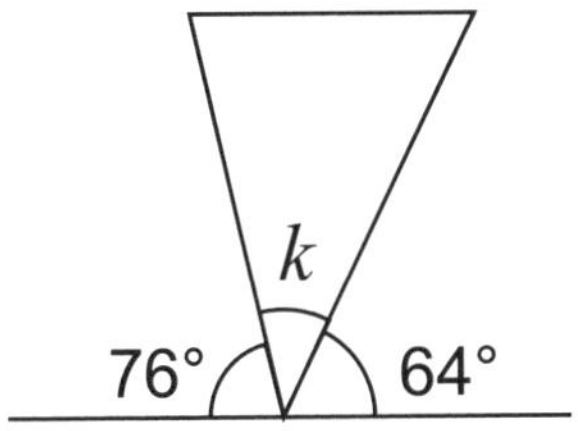

37. Joe rings 26 friends to invite them to his party. Phone calls cost 12p a minute to a landline and 25p a minute to a mobile phone. He rings 16 of his friends on their mobile phones and 10 of his friends on their landlines. Each phone call lasts for 2 minutes.

    How much will it cost him to phone all 26 friends?

    Answer: £ _____

38. Which pair of fractions are equivalent?

    A $8/12$ and $6/9$ C $4/12$ and $18/24$ E $10/18$ and $6/9$
    B $18/24$ and $6/9$ D $8/12$ and $18/24$

39. The diagram on the right shows the first 3 hexagons in a sequence.
    The hexagons are all regular.

    What is the perimeter of the 6th hexagon in the sequence?

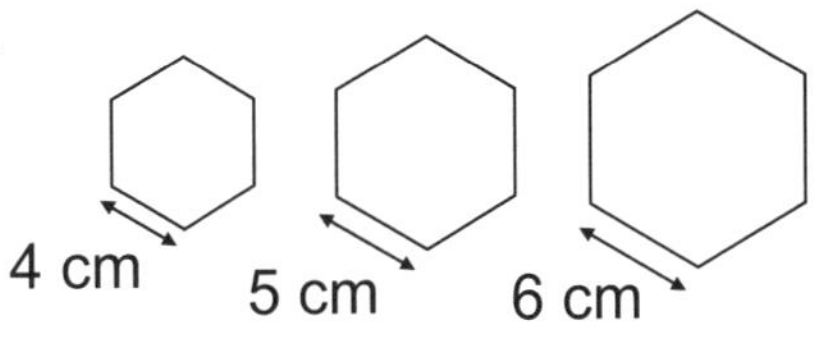

    Answer: _____ cm

40. Tom rides his bike twice as far as his brother, Lewis. Lewis rode Y miles.
    How far did both of them ride altogether?

    A 2Y   B 1 + 2Y   C Y × Y + 1   D 1.5Y   E 3Y

End of Test

Assessment Test 2

Assessment Test 3

Allow 40 minutes to do this test. Work as quickly and as carefully as you can.

You can print **multiple-choice answer sheets** for these questions from our website — go to cgpbooks.co.uk/11plus/answer-sheets or scan the QR code on the right. If you'd prefer to answer them in standard write-in format, either write your answers in the spaces provided or circle the **correct answer** from the options **A** to **E**.

1. What is the smallest number that can be made by writing the digits 5, 9 and 0 in these boxes? Use each digit only once.

    Answer: _____

2. The tally chart shows the points awarded to four teams in a quiz. How many points did Team 4 get?

    Answer: _____

Team	Number of Points
1	̷H̷H̷ ̷H̷H̷ ̷H̷H̷ II
2	̷H̷H̷ ̷H̷H̷ ̷H̷H̷ ̷H̷H̷ ̷H̷H̷ ̷H̷H̷ III
3	̷H̷H̷ ̷H̷H̷ ̷H̷H̷
4	̷H̷H̷ ̷H̷H̷ ̷H̷H̷ ̷H̷H̷ ̷H̷H̷ III

3. The 11 digits in Shazim's telephone number add up to 40. The last two digits add up to 10. Some of the digits in Shazim's telephone number are shown on the right.

    07070 3_642_

    What are the two missing digits?

    A 5 and 6 **C** 4 and 8 **E** 2 and 8
    B 4 and 7 **D** 3 and 8

4. A regular pentagon has a perimeter of 65 mm. What is the length of one side?   Answer: _____ mm

5. Look at the shape on the right. Which angle is a reflex angle?   Answer: _____

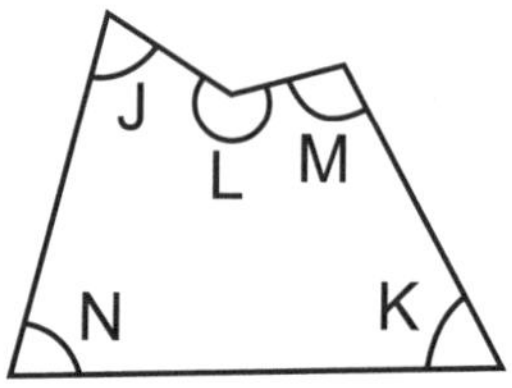

6. How many seconds are there in one hour?

    A 60   **B** 1440   **C** 1800   **D** 3600   **E** 2400

7. The table shows the films shown by a cinema in a year. Steph is 10 years old, and only watches action films or comedy films. She is only allowed to go and see films with a U or PG rating.

    How many different films could Steph go and watch at this cinema in a year?

    Answer: _____

Rating	Type of Film		
	Comedy	Drama	Action
U	15	14	7
PG	11	17	8
12	13	26	4
15	18	44	4

8. A shop has reduced the price of all its CDs by 20% in a sale. If CDs usually cost £10 each, how much will it cost to buy three CDs in the sale?

    Answer: £ _____

    / 8

9. Which of the following is 690?

   A 672 rounded to the nearest 100.
   B 683 rounded to the nearest 10.
   C 703 rounded to the nearest 10.
   D 694 rounded to the nearest 10.
   E 688.5 rounded to the nearest whole number.

10. Elsie is 4 years old and her grandmother is 4^3 years old.

    How many years older than Elsie is her grandmother?   Answer: _____

11. The temperature outside is −4 °C.
    The temperature inside is 28 °C warmer.

    Which thermometer shows
    the temperature inside?

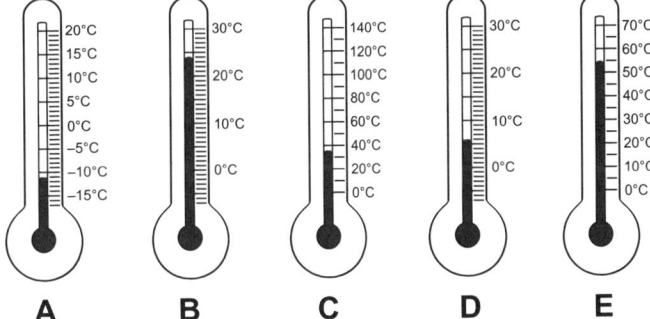

12. Kelly buys six eggs, two bottles of milk and
    one packet of cheese from the Farm Shop.
    What is the total cost?

    A £4.27   **C** £5.27   **E** £5.37
    B £4.97   **D** £6.97

    Farm Shop
    Eggs   6 for £1
    Rolls   69p each
    Milk   99p
    Cheese   £2.29

13. Victor uses white and black squares to make this pattern.

    How many black squares will he need
    to make the next shape in the pattern?   Answer: _____

14. Luke is thinking of a number. He gives these clues about his number:

    1. It is a multiple of 3.   2. It is a factor of 90.

    Which of the following could be Luke's number?

    A 24   **B** 16   **C** 4   **D** 30   **E** 10

15. Zuzanna drew this semi-circle on a grid.
    Each square on the grid is 1 cm².

    Which of the following is the best
    estimate for the area of the semi-circle?

    A 30 cm²   **D** 10 cm²
    B 20 cm²   **E** 35 cm²
    C 40 cm²

    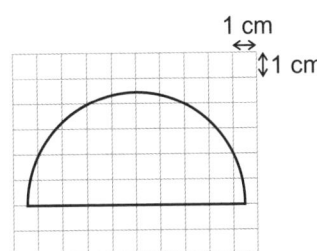

16. | 930 ÷ 5 = 186 |

   What is 310 ÷ 5?   Answer: _____

Colour	Number of Cars
Red	🚗 🚗
Black	🚗 🚗 🚗
Silver	🚗
Blue	🚗 🚗
White	🚗 🚗

🚗 = 2 cars

17. The pictogram on the right shows the colour of every car that passed a school in 10 minutes. What was the ratio of red cars to silver cars?

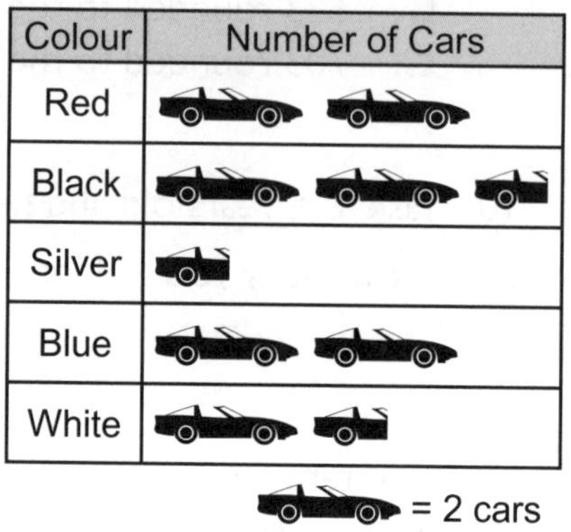

   Answer: _____ : _____

18. Z > 211.55
   Which of these numbers could be Z?
   A 210.95 **B** 209.99 **C** 211.48 **D** 122.66 **E** 211.7

19. What is the remainder when 709 is divided by 25?
   A 21 **B** 11 **C** 9 **D** 1 **E** 3

20. Which of these nets will not fold up to make a cuboid?

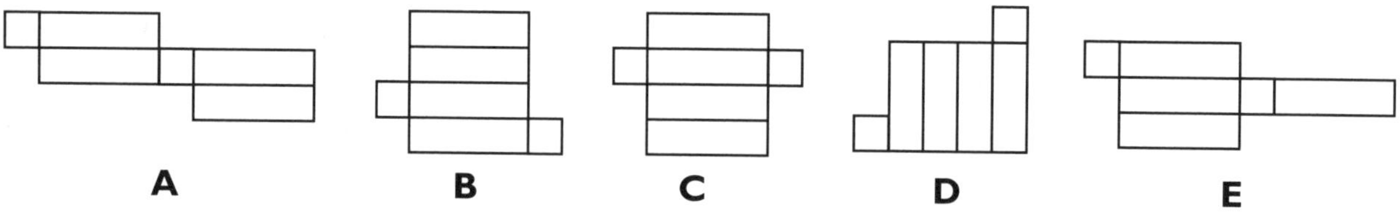

   A   B   C   D   E

21. Look at this sequence: 2.25, 1.75, 1.25, 0.75 ...
   What is the next number in this sequence?
   A 0.50 **B** −0.25 **C** −0.75 **D** 0.25 **E** 1.25

22. A candle burns down by 2 cm every 13 minutes.
   How many minutes will a 30 cm candle burn for?
   A 260 minutes   **C** 200 minutes   **E** 780 minutes
   B 195 minutes   **D** 300 minutes

23. A return bus ticket to the museum costs 25p for a child and 99p for an adult. 24 children are going to the museum with 3 teachers.

   What is the total cost of the bus fares?

   Answer: £ _____

24. A watering can holds two litres of water.
   Jo has 100 tomato plants and each plant needs 160 ml of water.

   How many times will Jo have to fill the watering can to water all of the plants?

   Answer: _____

/ 9

Assessment Test 3

25. Clayton built the model on the right using cubes.
    Which of the options shows his model viewed from the back?

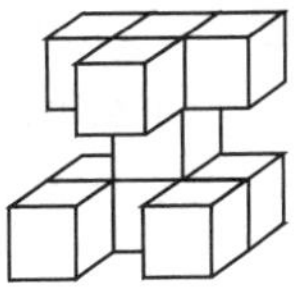

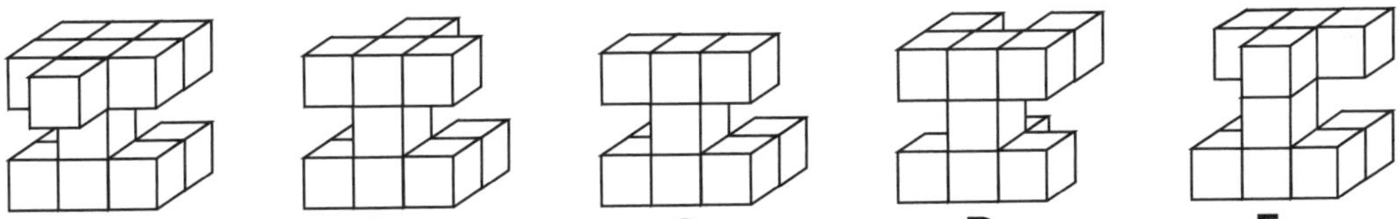

    A   B   C   D   E

26. A recipe for 24 fairy cakes needs 200 g of butter. Joe has a 2.5 kg pack of butter.
    How many fairy cakes is this enough for?

    A   250   C   96   E   300
    B   500   D   144

27. The clock on the right shows the time five past twelve.
    Between this time and twenty-five past twelve,
    what angle will the minute hand turn through?

    Answer: _____ °

28. The graph on the right shows a family's journey
    through four towns.
    How far did they travel between Town C and Town D?

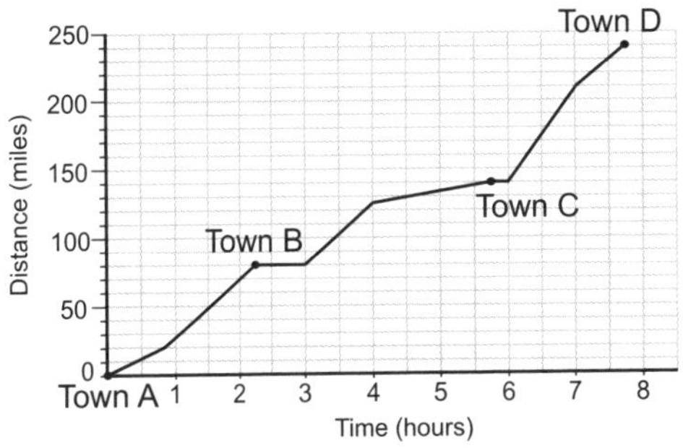

    Answer: _____ miles

29. A box contains chocolate bars with a total weight of 1.4 kg. Each bar of chocolate weighs 70 g.
    How many chocolate bars are there in the box?

    A   25   B   70   C   20   D   16   E   2

30. This list shows the number of words in some maths questions: 27, 33, 38, 26
    What is the mean number of words in a question?

    A   25   B   28   C   31   D   32   E   27

31. Megan places two dice on top of each other on a table as shown.
    The number of dots on the opposite faces of each dice add up to 7.
    She can see eight side faces and the face on the top.
    Megan counts all of the dots on the faces she can see.

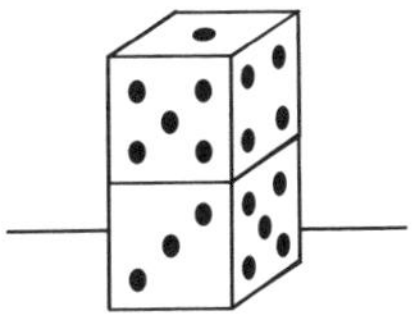

    How many dots does she count?

    Answer: _____

32. A fridge uses 0.6 units of electricity each hour.
    How much electricity will it use if it is switched on for 150 hours?

    Answer: _____ units

/ 8

Carry on to the next question → →

Assessment Test 3

33. This path is made of circular paving stones which are all the same size. $\frac{1}{3}$ of some of the paving stones are grey. What fraction of the path is grey?

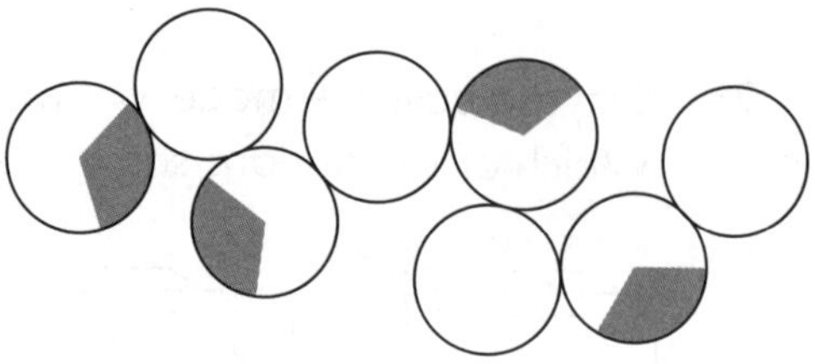

   A $\frac{1}{3}$ B $\frac{2}{4}$ C $\frac{2}{10}$ D $\frac{1}{6}$ E $\frac{1}{4}$

34. A packet of sweets contains 4 orange sweets and 3 green sweets. Jane wants to decorate a cake. She wants to use a green sweet first and then alternate the colours until she has used 20 sweets.

   How many packets of sweets does she need to buy?   Answer: _____

35. A leaking pipe drips once every 12 seconds. It takes 3 hours for the water to fill a 12 litre bowl.

   How much water is lost from the pipe in one day?

   Answer: _____ litres

36. The triangle on this coordinate grid is reflected in the mirror line. What are the coordinates of corner A after the reflection?

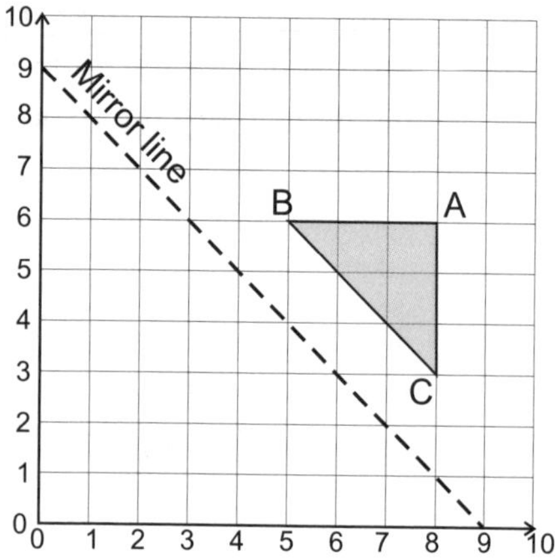

   Answer: (____, ____)

37. A cube with sides of 10 cm holds one litre of water. How many litres of water could be held in a cuboid with sides of 80 cm, 20 cm and 1 m?

   Answer: _____ litres

38. The pie chart on the right shows the proportion of children wearing hats, scarves and gloves to school.
   Approximately what percentage of children are wearing gloves?

   A 50%   B 60%   C 30%   D 90%   E 75%

39. The rectangular faces of this octagonal prism each have an area of R and the octagonal faces each have an area of C.
   Which expression shows the total area of all the faces of this octagonal prism?

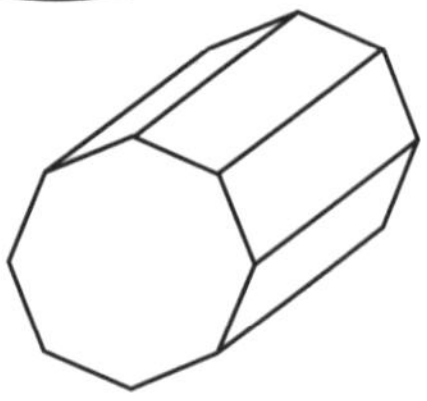

   A 4R + 4C   C 6R + 2C   E 2R + 6C
   B 8R + 2C   D R + C

40. Shannon and Ray measure the perimeter of a rectangular field. The tape measure they use is 27 m long. Along the length of the field, the tape measure fits four times. Along the width of the field, the tape measure fits twice.

   What is the perimeter of the field?

   Answer: _____ m

/ 8

End of Test

Assessment Test 3

Assessment Test 4

Allow 40 minutes to do this test. Work as quickly and as carefully as you can.

You can print **multiple-choice answer sheets** for these questions from our website — go to cgpbooks.co.uk/11plus/answer-sheets or scan the QR code on the right. If you'd prefer to answer them in standard write-in format, either write your answers in the spaces provided or circle the **correct answer** from the options **A** to **E**.

1. Which of these is the smallest number?

    A 0.57　　**B** 16.01　　**C** 1.63　　**D** 0.23　　**E** 8.1

2. The table on the right shows when five children were born. Who is the youngest?

    Answer: _____

	Month	Year
Archie	June	1999
Damien	January	1999
Sara	May	1997
Hamid	December	1999
Mena	February	1997

3. Rearrange the digits in 27 149 to make the largest even number possible.

    Answer: _____

4. How many millimetres are there in 3.5 metres?

    A 35　　**B** 350　　**C** 3050　　**D** 3500　　**E** 35 000

5. The three lines on the right are reflected in a mirror line to form a shape. What shape is made?

    A rectangle　　**C** pentagon　　**E** hexagon
    B quadrilateral　　**D** rhombus

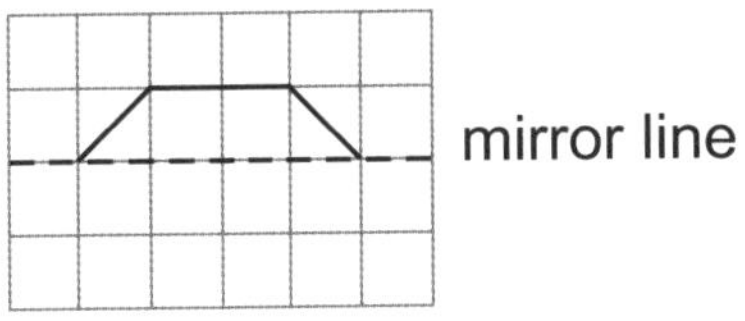

6. Liam divides a number by 5. He is left with a remainder of 3. Which of the following could have been his original number?

    A 42　　**B** 17　　**C** 23　　**D** 9　　**E** 21

7. In a sale a dress is reduced by 25%. The original price was £16. What is the sale price?

    Answer: £_____

8. The graph shows the number of books borrowed from the school library over four days. What was the mean number of books borrowed?

    Answer: _____

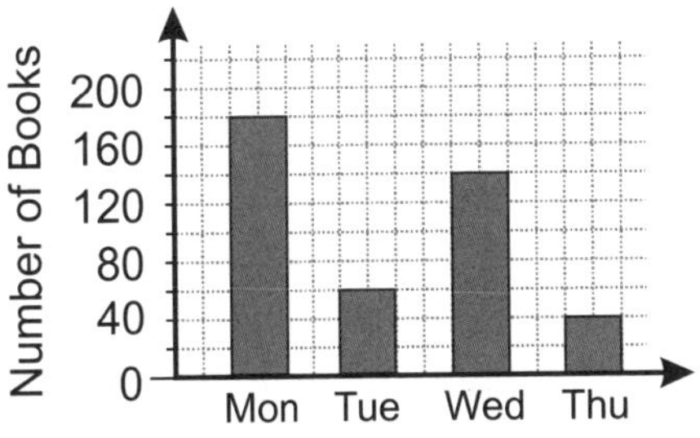

9. How many fifths are there in 5?

    A 25　　**B** 5　　**C** 1　　**D** 21　　**E** 17

/ 9

Carry on to the next question → →

10. Salma buys a bag of apples for £2.50. There are 10 apples in the bag.
    How much does each apple cost?

    Answer: _____ p

11. Look at the shape on the right.
    Which two lines are perpendicular?

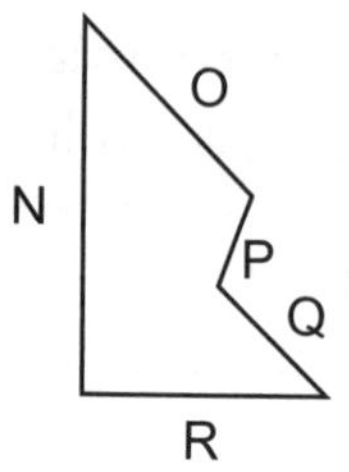

    A N and O   **C** N and R   **E** Q and P
    B Q and R   **D** O and Q

12. Estimate the size of angle *y*.

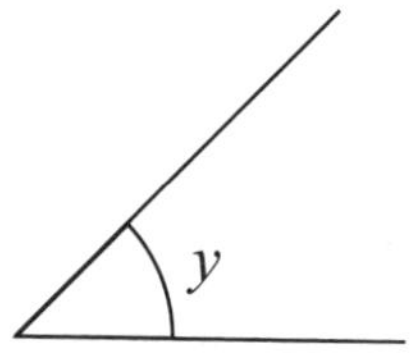

    A 45°   **C** 75°   **E** 10°
    B 90°   **D** 20°

13. The temperature in Hameed's garden is −3 °C.
    The temperature in Hameed's kitchen is 21 °C.

    What is the difference between the two temperatures?

    Answer: _____ °C

14. The colours of the front doors of houses in a street were recorded in a pictogram.
    How many more black doors were there than blue ones?

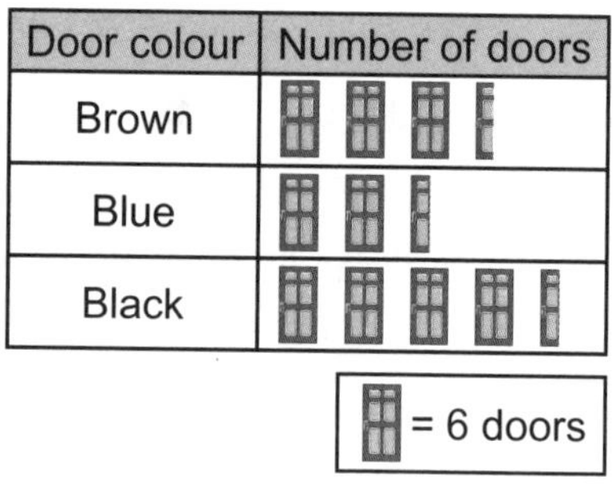

    Answer: _____

Door colour	Number of doors
Brown	
Blue	
Black	

    = 6 doors

15. Which of the following statements could be true?

    A A guinea pig weighs 17.5 g   **D** A guinea pig weighs 7 g
    B A guinea pig weighs 750 g   **E** A guinea pig weighs 700 kg
    C A guinea pig weighs 75 kg

16. The diagram shows a rectangular school playground.
    Chris ran around the perimeter of the playground twice.

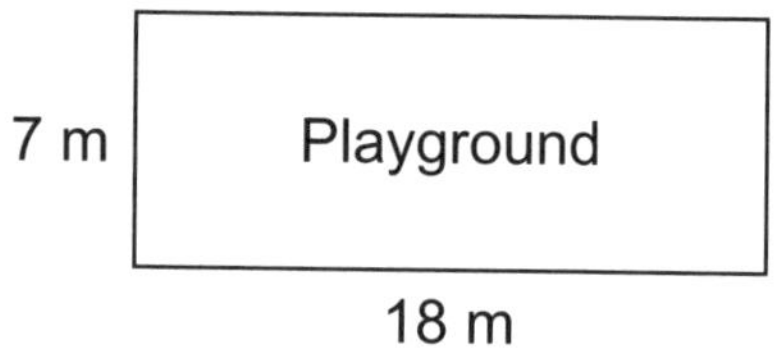

    How many metres did Chris run?

    Answer: _____ m

    7 m   Playground
    18 m

17. 234 ÷ 9 = 26

    What is 468 ÷ 9?   Answer: _____

18. Pat multiplies a number by 4. She then squares the result. The number she ends up with is 64.
    What number did Pat start with?

    A 2   **B** 4   **C** 8   **D** 32   **E** 16

/ 9

Assessment Test 4

19. The diagram shows a weighing scale.
    What weight will the scale show
    if the pointer rotates 270° clockwise?

    Answer: _____ kg

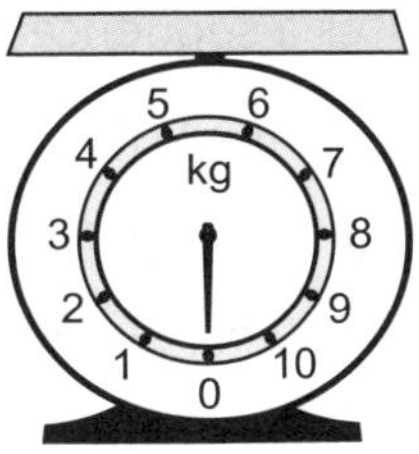

20. What is 20.7 × 6?

    A 138.6   **B** 120.42   **C** 116.4   **D** 124.2   **E** 136.8

21. Daud asked the children in his class whether
    they like Chinese, Indian and Italian food.
    The Venn diagram shows their answers.

    How many children in total like both Chinese and Italian food?

    Answer: _____

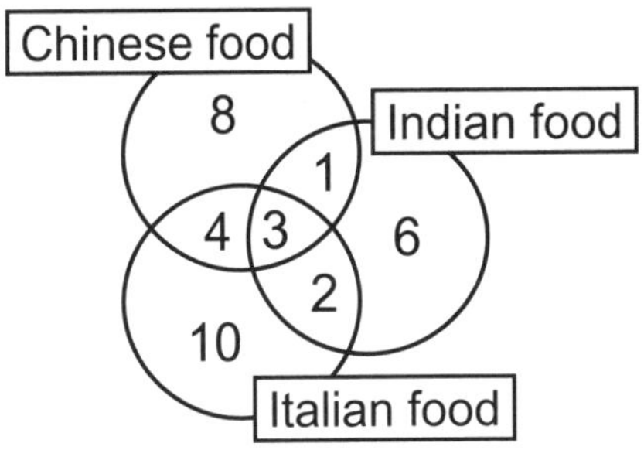

22. A recipe to make 10 pies requires 200 g of flour.
    How much flour would be needed to make 15 pies?

    Answer: _____ g

23. The table shows the number of goals scored by
    the teams taking part in a netball tournament.

Number of goals	1	2	3	4	5
Number of teams	3	2	2	2	1

    What percentage of the teams scored more than two goals?

    Answer: _____ %

24. A newspaper has forty pages.
    The sports pages make up two-fifths of the paper.

    How many pages are not sports pages?   Answer: _____

25. A parking space for a car needs to be 5 m long and 3 m wide.
    The car park on the right is used for three spaces.

    What area of the car park is left over?

    Answer: _____ m²

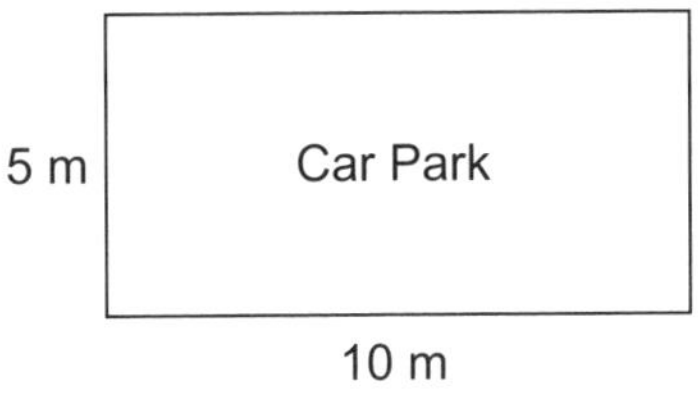

26. It takes Jeanne 1 minute to walk from her house to the park.
    It then takes $5\frac{1}{2}$ minutes for Jeanne to walk from the park to her school.

    How many seconds does it take Jeanne to get to school from her house?

    Answer: _____ seconds

Carry on to the next question → →

Assessment Test 4

27. Martha writes a sequence of numbers with the rule:

    Subtract 2 from the last number and then double it.

    The first four numbers in the sequence are:

        5, 6, 8, 12

    What is the 6th number in Martha's sequence?　　　Answer: _____

28. Which of these sets of numbers has the greatest mean?

    A   6, 8, 8, 9, 9   **C**   2, 4, 8, 5, 6   **E**   7, 5, 12, 5, 6
    B   8, 4, 9, 5, 4   **D**   4, 4, 8, 10, 9

29. Alice has twelve chocolates.
    Three of the chocolates are coffee creams. The rest are strawberry creams.

    What is the ratio of coffee creams to strawberry creams? Simplify your answer.

    Answer: _____ : _____

30. Which of the following points is not inside the shaded circle?

    A   (8, 4)   **C**   (2, 3)   **E**   (5, 3)
    B   (6, 6)   **D**   (4, 7)

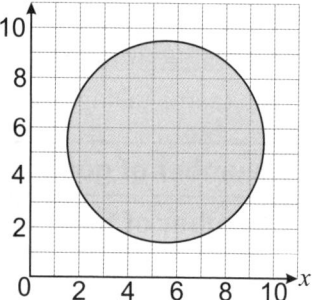

31. Rodrigo has three 1.5 litre bottles of water.
    He pours the water into 250 ml glasses.

    How many glasses can he fill with his bottles of water?

    A   20   **B**   15   **C**   30   **D**   8   **E**   18

32. The bar chart shows the number of lengths of a swimming pool that some of the children in a class swam.

    How many children did not swim if there are 30 children in the class altogether?

    A   9   **C**   29   **E**   12
    B   1   **D**   5

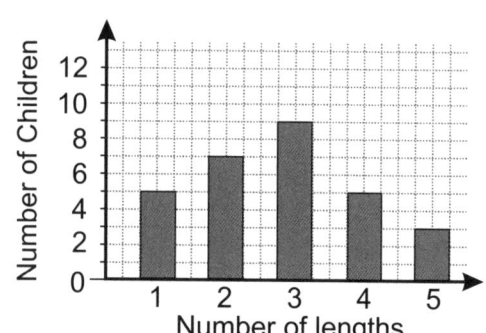

33. Manjit buys six cartons of apple juice. She pays with a ten pound note and receives £2.80 in change.

    How much does each carton of apple juice cost?

    Answer: £ _____

34. Some people were asked where they went on holiday.
    The results were recorded in a pie chart.

    12 people went to Turkey.
    How many people did not go to Turkey?

    Answer: _____

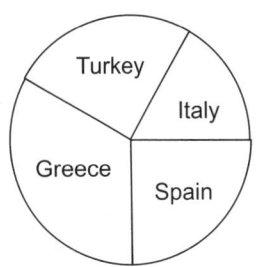

35. The wooden block shown on the right is a cuboid.
    What is its volume?

    A   16 cm³   C   32 cm³   E   5 cm³
    B   40 cm³   D   20 cm³

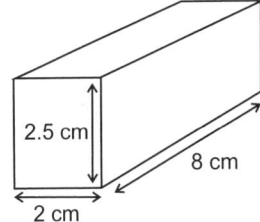

36. This is a bus timetable from Blackford to Birmingham.

Blackford	10:00	10:30	11:00	11:30	12:00
Henley	10:45	11:15	11:45	12:15	12:45
Dunny-on-the-Wold	11:30	12:00	12:30	13:00	13:30
Birmingham	12:00	12:30	13:00	13:30	14:00

    Ahmed lives in Henley and his home is ten minutes walk from
    the bus stop. He wants to arrive in Birmingham by 13:15.

    What is the latest time that Ahmed should leave his home?

    A   11:45   B   11:15   C   11:35   D   12:05   E   10:45

37. Maddy starts at 10 and counts back in steps of $2\frac{1}{4}$.
    Which of these numbers will she count?

    A   5   B   4   C   3   D   2   E   1

38. What is the size of angle *h*?

    Answer: _____°

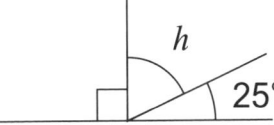

39. The circumference of a wheel is 85.5 cm. It is rolled
    along a corridor. The wheel makes 7 complete turns.

    How far does it roll?

    A   585.5 cm   C   558 cm   E   598.5 cm
    B   590 cm   D   625.5 cm

40. Magdalena buys two dresses. One costs £X and the other costs £Y.
    She also buys three blouses which each cost £Z.

    Which expression shows the total amount that she spends in pounds?

    A   X + Y + 3Z   C   3Z   E   2X + 2Y + 3Z
    B   X + Y + Z   D   X + Y

End of Test

Assessment Test 4

Assessment Test 5

Allow 40 minutes to do this test. Work as quickly and as carefully as you can.

You can print **multiple-choice answer sheets** for these questions from our website — go to cgpbooks.co.uk/11plus/answer-sheets or scan the QR code on the right. If you'd prefer to answer them in standard write-in format, either write your answers in the spaces provided or circle the **correct answer** from the options **A** to **E**.

1. What is 5 × 3000? Answer: _____

2. Topi has 136 DVDs. She wants to store them all on shelves. She can fit fifty DVDs on each shelf.

   How many shelves does Topi need to store all the DVDs? Answer: _____

3. What are the coordinates of corner C on this triangle?

   Answer: (_____ , _____)

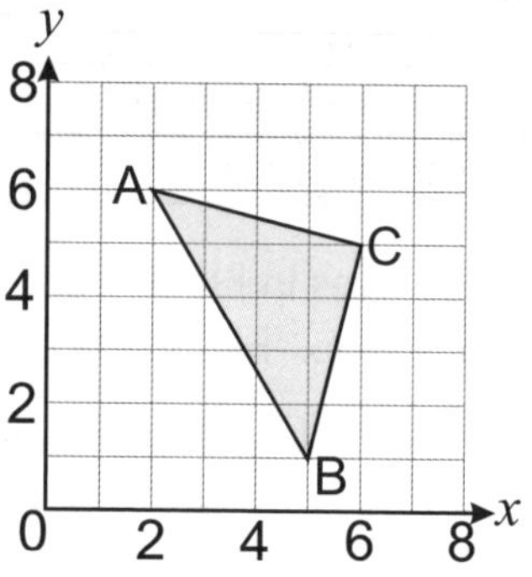

4. Chloe is 4 years old.
   Which of these is most likely to be her height?

   A 40 cm   **C** 0.5 km   **E** 90 cm
   B 80 mm   **D** 2 m

5. The table shows the weekly pocket money for the children in a class.

   For this class, what is the difference between the maximum amount of weekly pocket money and the minimum amount?

Weekly pocket money	Number of children
50p	3
£1.00	8
£1.50	7
£2.00	6
£2.50	4

   Answer: £ _____

6. The diagram shows a weighing scale. What weight does the pointer show?

   Answer: _____ kg

7. There are 25 pencils in a box. A box of pencils costs £4.99. How much does it cost to buy 75 pencils?

   Answer: £ _____

8. A school is planning to build a small swimming pool. Which unit would be best to use to measure the volume of water needed to fill the pool?

   A kg   **B** km³   **C** m   **D** m³   **E** ml

/ 8

9. Mrs Brown gives her cat two packets of food each day. The food comes in boxes of 24 packets. How many boxes does Mrs Brown need to buy to feed her cat for three weeks?

   Answer: _____

10. The diagram shows a set of steps. All the steps are the same size. Mr Ogun has some spare lengths of carpet. Which length of carpet will be enough to cover all the steps with the least amount left over?

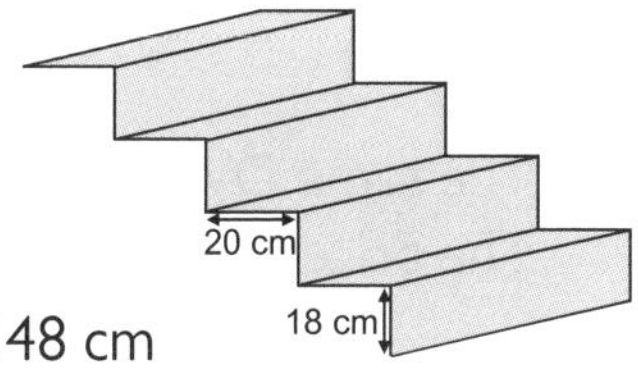

    A 180 cm   **B** 100 cm   **C** 160 cm   **D** 130 cm   **E** 148 cm

11. Look at the diagram. Which of the following describes the route from the supermarket to the chemist?

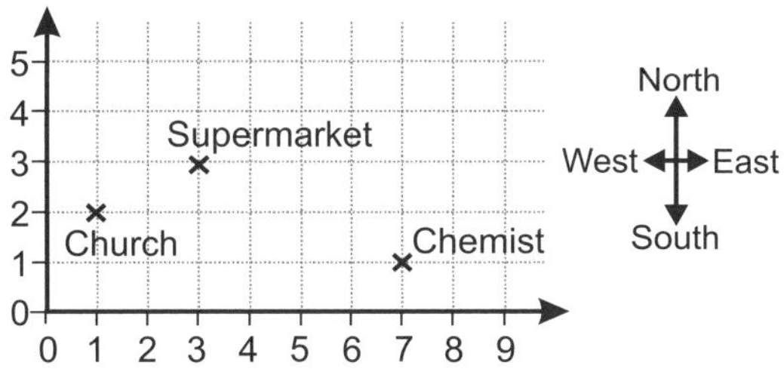

    A 4 squares west, 2 squares north
    B 2 squares west, 1 square south
    C 3 squares south, 1 square east
    D 4 squares east, 2 squares south
    E 2 squares south, 4 squares west

12. How many fifths are there in $6^2/_5$?   Answer: _____

13. Halima counts backwards from 39 in steps of 9. Which of these numbers will she count?

    A 7   **B** 6   **C** 5   **D** 4   **E** 3

14. The diagram shows part of a juice bar menu. What is the ratio of the number of drinks that contain banana to the total number of drinks on the menu?

    A 2 : 5   **B** 3 : 5   **C** 2 : 3   **D** 3 : 2   **E** 1 : 5

    Jolly Juice Bar
    MENU

Drink	Contains
Pink Fizz	Raspberry, Banana
Lemon Zing	Lemon, Orange
Fairy Drink	Orange, Kiwi
Redberry punch	Strawberry, Banana
Apple Fizz	Apple, Orange

15. What is 99 − 0.18?

    Answer: _____

16. What fraction of this shape is shaded?

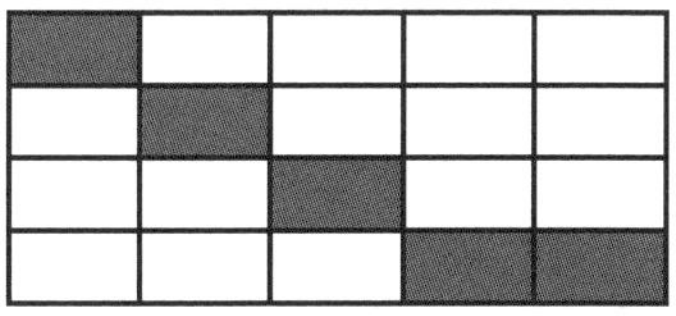

    A $\frac{2}{3}$ **B** $\frac{1}{5}$ **C** $\frac{1}{4}$ **D** $\frac{1}{2}$ **E** $\frac{1}{3}$

17. Lucy buys four friends a chocolate bar each. Each bar costs 89p. How much change will she get if she pays for the chocolate bars with a five pound note?

    Answer: £ _____

18. Orla wants to turf her garden.
    A roll of turf is 4 m long and 1 m wide.

    How many rolls of turf does Orla need to buy?

    Answer: _____

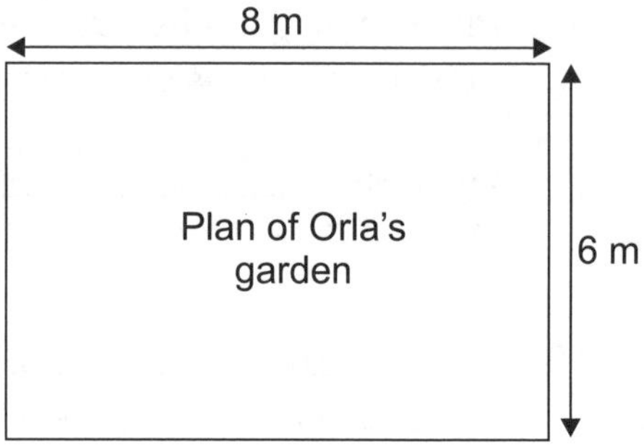

    Plan of Orla's garden — 8 m by 6 m

19. The same DVD is sold at different prices in five shops.
    The prices are £12.50, £13.00, £10.00, £15.00 and £9.50.

    What is the mean price of the DVD?

    Answer: £ _____

20. Which of these numbers is the smallest?

    A 1⅕   B 1¼   C 1.05   D 1.5   E 1.25

21. Hayley counts the number of cars of different colours in the school car park. She works out that 25% of the cars are red. If there are four red cars, how many cars are there in total in the car park?

    Answer: _____

22. Which of the following shapes should be put in the shaded box of the sorting table?

    A square   D rectangle
    B right-angled triangle   E parallelogram
    C equilateral triangle

	At least 2 equal sides	No equal sides
Obtuse angles	▓▓▓	
No obtuse angles		

23. A cinema charges £3.55 for entry before 6 pm and £5.45 after 6 pm.
    Mrs Jones goes to the cinema after 6 pm three times a month.
    How much would Mrs Jones save each month by going before 6 pm instead?

    Answer: £ _____

24. Which numbers on this diagram are divisible by both 3 and 5?

    A 42, 75, 135   C 42, 75   E 75, 135
    B 135, 42   D 25, 75, 135

    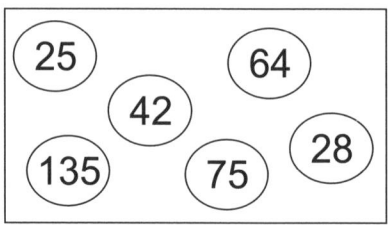

25. The table shows the pets that children in a class have. Three children have two different pets.

    How many children are there in the class?

    Answer: _____

Pet	Number of children
Cat	8
Dog	6
Guinea pig	4
Rabbit	2
Mouse	1
None	12

    / 8

26. This line graph converts fuel consumption in km per litre to miles per gallon.
Mr Khan buys a new car with a fuel consumption of 15 km per litre.

How many miles per gallon is this?

Answer: _____ miles per gallon

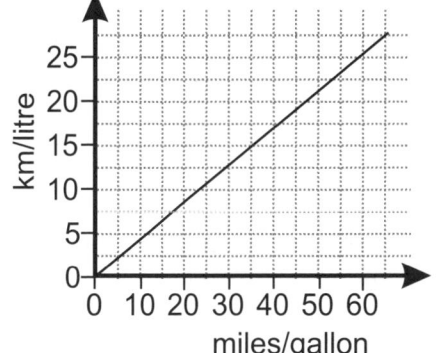

27. Andrew sells scones for £1 each on his stall at the market. It costs him 52p to make each scone. How much profit does he make if he sells 80 scones?

Answer: £ _____

28. The table shows some information given on the label on a tin of baked beans.

How many grams of carbohydrate would a 1 kg tin of baked beans contain?

Answer: _____ g

	Typical values per 100 g
Protein	4.4 g
Fat	0.6 g
Carbohydrate	13.4 g
Fibre	4.2 g

29. Ali has written this sequence of numbers: 4, 8, 16, 32 ……
What is the sixth term in this sequence?

Answer: _____

30. The diagram shows a triangle. Two of the angles in the triangle are given. What is the size of the third angle?

Answer: _____ °

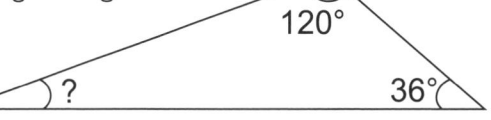

31. Icebury tomato ketchup is sold in five different sizes. Which of these sizes gives the best value for money?

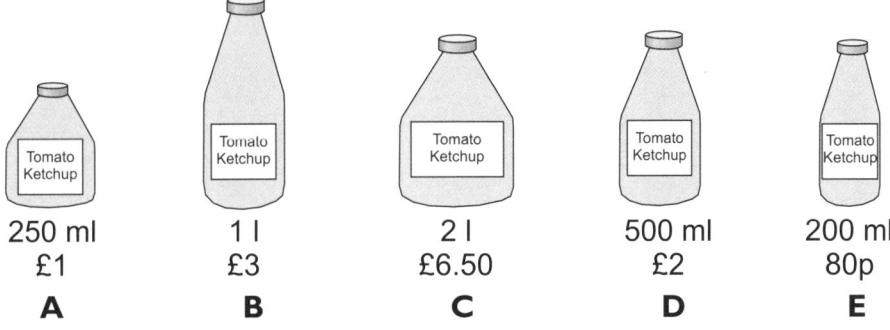

250 ml	1 l	2 l	500 ml	200 ml
£1	£3	£6.50	£2	80p
A	B	C	D	E

32. Michelle finds that 5% of the sweets in a packet are red. If there are 3 red sweets in the packet, how many sweets are there altogether?

Answer: _____

/ 7

Carry on to the next question → →

33. The pie chart shows how Sunita spends the 24 hours of Saturday.
How many hours does Sunita spend running?

   A 2   B 4   C 3   D 5   E 6

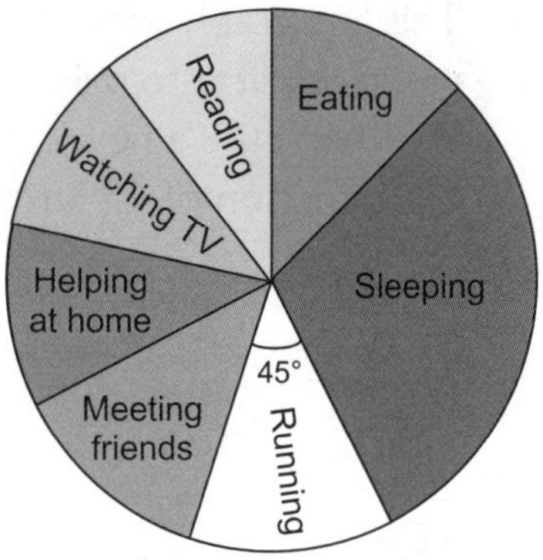

34. Aisha has ten books. They are all 20 cm × 9 cm × 0.5 cm.
She has a box which the ten books fit into exactly.

   What is the volume of the box?

   Answer: _____ cm³

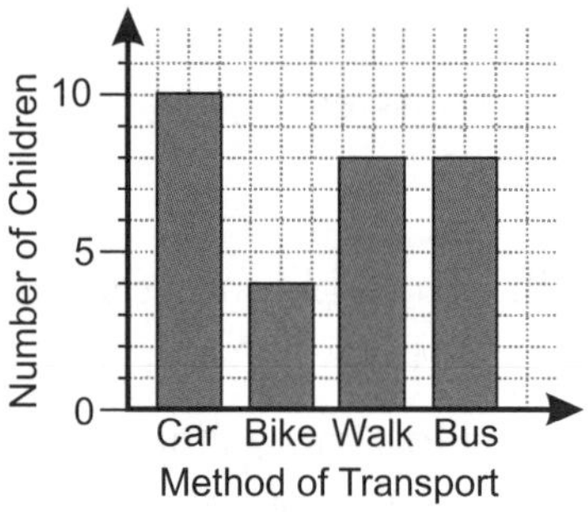

35. This bar chart shows how the children in one class travel to school.
What fraction of the children go to school by car?

   A ⅔   B ⅝   C ½   D ⅓   E ¼

36. Each of the 5 members of the Brown family take two chicken sandwiches for lunch on 5 days of the week. Each sandwich contains 40 g of chicken. If 1 kg of chicken costs £6.49, how much will they spend on chicken each week?

   Answer: £ _____

37. Sam puts six songs on his MP3 player. The lengths of the songs are 2 mins, 3 mins, 2 mins, 2 mins, 2 mins and 4 mins.

   What is the mean length of the songs in minutes?

   A 2 mins   B 4 mins   C 3.5 mins   D 2.5 mins   E 3 mins

38. 1 mile = 1.6 km
The distance from Paris to Nice by road is 600 miles.

   Which of these is the nearest to the distance from Paris to Nice in kilometres?

   A 1000 km   B 600 km   C 400 km   D 800 km   E 1200 km

39. **56 × 946 = 52 976**. What is 946 × 28?   Answer: _____

40. The Singh family book a minibus to the airport.
There is a booking charge of £12, then a charge of £2 per mile.

   Which expression gives the cost in pounds for a journey that is y miles long?

   A $12y$ B $12y + 2$ C $14y + 12$ D $14 + 2y$ E $12 + 2y$

/ 8

End of Test

Assessment Test 5

Answers

Section One — Number Knowledge
Page 2

Count how many places the digit is from the left or right of the decimal point.

1) **Tens or six tens**
The digit is two places to the left of the decimal point.
This is the tens column.

2) **Thousands or three thousand**
The digit is four places to the left of the decimal point.
This is the thousands column.

3) **Hundredths or three hundredths**
The digit is two places to the right of the decimal point.
This is the hundredths column.

4) **Tenths or four tenths**
The digit is one place to the right of the decimal point.
This is the tenths column.

5) **Thousandths or one thousandth**
The digit is three places to the right of the decimal point.
This is the thousandths column.

Compare the place value of the digits in the options. Start with the value of the digits on the left of the decimal point. If these have the same place value and are the same number, compare the values of the next lot of digits to the right until you find the smallest number and place value.

6) **1.62**   7) **3.02**
8) **123.7**   9) **1.27**
10) **0.144**

11) **8 017 452**
Think about the place value columns and which words go into which columns. Be careful — there are no hundred thousands, so you need to put a zero in that column.

Find the difference between the two given numbers on a number line. Divide the difference by the number of sections the number line is split into to find how much the number line increases by at each point.

12) **70**
Each mark on the number line is worth 5.

13) **28.6**
Each mark on the number line is worth 0.2.

14) **Jack**
The biggest number will be the slowest time. Compare the place value of the digits in the options. Start with the value of the digits on the left of the decimal point. If these have the same place value and are the same number, compare the values of the next lot of digits to the right until you find the biggest number and place value. The biggest number is 14.4.

15) **5.11 and 4.89**
Find the difference between 5 and each number in the pairs given.
5.11 – 5 = 0.11
5 – 4.89 = 0.11

Page 3

Look at the digit to the right of the digit you're rounding. If it's 5 or more you round up, if it's less than 5 you round down.

1) **790**
8 is being rounded, 6 is greater than 5, so 786 rounds up to 790.

2) **900**
8 is being rounded, 5 is equal to 5, so 851 rounds up to 900.

3) **2400**
4 is being rounded, 2 is less than 5,
so 2421 rounds down to 2400.

4) **9000**
8 is being rounded, 5 is equal to 5, so 8578 rounds up to 9000.

5) **4000**
4 is being rounded, 4 is less than 5,
so 4426 rounds down to 4000.

6) **nearest 100**
3 is being rounded, 5 is equal to 5, so 355 rounds up to 400.

7) **nearest 10**
7 is being rounded, 8 is greater than 5,
so 278 rounds up to 280.

8) **nearest 10**
8 is being rounded, 2 is less than 5,
so 3682 rounds down to 3680.

9) **nearest 1000**
4 is being rounded, 3 is less than 5,
so 4367 rounds down to 4000.

10) **nearest 100**
4 is being rounded, 6 is greater than 5,
so 3469 rounds up to 3500.

11) **27 600**
6 is being rounded, 4 is less than 5,
so 27 642 rounds down to 27 600.

12) **176**
5 is being rounded, 6 is greater than 5,
so 175.639 rounds up to 176.

13) **100.4 g**
3 is being rounded, 6 is greater than 5,
so 100.364 rounds up to 100.4.

14) **160 cm**
To round 159.67 cm to the nearest whole centimetre you need to round the digit in the units column. 9 is being rounded, 6 is greater than 5, so 159.67 cm rounds up to 160 cm. 9 tens rounds up to 10 tens — the '0' stays in the units column and the '1' gets carried over to the tens column.

15) **C**
Round the number given in each option until you find the one that rounds to 1000.
C: 956 — 9 is being rounded, 5 is equal to 5,
so 956 rounds up to 1000. C is the correct answer.

Pages 4-5

The biggest negative number will have the smallest value. It will be the furthest left on a number line.

1) −5
2) −9
3) −28
4) −30
5) −1

6) 98
The only number that is greater than 68 is 98.

7) 64.5
The only number which is less than 65 and greater than 64 is 64.5.

8) 21
The only number which is greater than 20 and less than 22 is 21.

9) −11
The only number that is greater than −12 and less than −8 is −11.

10) 6.65
The only number which is less than 6.9 and greater than 6.5 is 6.65.

11) E
28 is both a multiple of 7 and an even number, so it should be in the part of the Venn diagram where the two sections overlap.

12) 6 > −3 + 9
−3 + 9 = 6. 6 is equal to 6, so the statement 6 > −3 + 9 is incorrect.

13) 24
24 is the only number that you can divide by both 3 and 4 to get a whole number. 24 ÷ 3 = 8. 24 ÷ 4 = 6.

14) D
The total score for D would be the sum of 3 odd numbers, which would give an odd number (13 + 21 + 57 = 91), so the answer is D.

15) A
2^3 = 8. The next cube number after 8 is 3^3 = 27, which is 19 greater than 8. So the answer is 2.

16) 6
The only number that 18 and 24 can be divided by to get a whole number is 6. 18 ÷ 6 = 3. 24 ÷ 6 = 4.

17) 17
The prime numbers between 1 and 10 are 2, 3, 5 and 7. So 2 + 3 + 5 + 7 = 17.

18) 24
The largest prime number below 20 is 19. 19 + 5 = 24.

19) E
29 is a prime number. 36 is a square number (6^2 = 36) and 42 is a multiple of 6 (6 × 7 = 42).

20) C
Both numbers need to be square numbers and multiples of 8. 16 and 64 are square numbers, 4^2 = 16, 8^2 = 64. 16 and 64 are both multiples of 8, 8 × 2 = 16, 8 × 8 = 64.

21) E
E is the only list with only odd numbers and no prime numbers.

22) 3
3 is both a factor of 18 which is less than 10 and a prime number which is less than 10.

23) C
The factors of 36 are 1, 2, 3, 4, 6, 9, 12, 18 and 36. You need to find the two numbers which add up to one of these numbers. 3 + 15 = 18, so the answer is C.

24) 55 years
3^2 = 9, 8^2 = 64, so 64 − 9 = 55 years.

25) D
M = 1000, C = 100, L = 50, X = 10 and I = 1. A smaller numeral before a larger one represents the difference between the two, so CM = 1000 − 100 = 900, XL = 50 − 10 = 40 and IX = 10 − 1 = 9. So the year is: 1000 + 900 + 40 + 9 = 1949.

Page 6

To find the rule in a sequence, try to find how to get from one number to another. It can help to look at the difference between the numbers, or try to spot a pattern, e.g. the numbers double each time.

1) 40
The rule of the sequence is add 8.

2) 15
The rule of the sequence is subtract 3.

3) 99
The rule of the sequence is add 22.

4) 96
The rule of the sequence is add 12.

5) 20 000
The rule of the sequence is multiply by 10.

6) 10
The sequence is 1, 4, 7, 10...

7) 8
The sequence is 1, 2, 4, 8...

8) 3
The sequence is −3, −1, 1, 3...

9) −4
The sequence is 20, 12, 4, −4...

10) 10
The sequence is 2.5, 5, 7.5, 10...

11) 18
The number of blocks on the bottom row increases by 3 with each row that is added, so the sequence goes 3, 6, 9, 12, 15, 18... The 6th number in the sequence is 18, so there will be 18 blocks on the bottom row of a tower that has 6 rows.

12) 8
Count back in 5s from 38 until you find a number between 5 and 10: 38, 33, 28, 23, 18, 13, 8

13) E
The only option that works is 12 and 48. The rule of the sequence is double the previous number: 3, 6, 12, 24, 48...

14) 1 and 4.75
The rule of the given numbers is to add 0.75 each time. So 1 and 4.75 would fit the sequence: 1, 1.75, 2.5, 3.25, 4, 4.75

Answers

15) Saturday
You can make a sequence where you start at 13 tins and subtract 3 tins each time. Remember, she has already fed her dogs on Monday, so start counting from Tuesday.

Tue	Wed	Thu	Fri	Sat
13	10	7	4	1

She'll run out of dog food on Saturday.

Page 7

Count the total number of parts and the number of shaded parts for each shape to work out the fraction. Remember to simplify your fractions where you can.

1) B
1 out of 3 parts of circle B is shaded = $\frac{1}{3}$.

2) E
One quarter of circle E is shaded = $\frac{1}{4}$.

3) D
$\frac{9}{14}$ of rectangle D is shaded.

4) A
$\frac{6}{15}$ of rectangle A is shaded.

5) C
Star C has 6 spikes.
One out of six of the spikes are shaded = $\frac{1}{6}$.

6) 4
$\frac{1}{6}$ of 24. 24 ÷ 6 = 4, 4 × 1 = 4

7) 6
$\frac{1}{4}$ of 24. 24 ÷ 4 = 6, 6 × 1 = 6

8) 2
$\frac{1}{12}$ of 24. 24 ÷ 12 = 2, 2 × 1 = 2

9) 3
$\frac{1}{8}$ of 24. 24 ÷ 8 = 3, 3 × 1 = 3

10) 9
$\frac{3}{8}$ of 24. 24 ÷ 8 = 3, 3 × 3 = 9

11) D
There are 4 boys and if they split the doughnuts equally then they will each get $\frac{1}{4}$ of the doughnuts.

12) $\frac{5}{6}$
To compare fractions, give them all a common denominator:
$\frac{1}{2} = \frac{6}{12}$, $\frac{5}{12} = \frac{5}{12}$, $\frac{2}{3} = \frac{8}{12}$, $\frac{5}{6} = \frac{10}{12}$ and $\frac{1}{3} = \frac{4}{12}$.
The biggest out of these fractions is $\frac{10}{12}$, so the answer is $\frac{5}{6}$.

13) 55
There are five fifths in 1 ($\frac{5}{5} = 1$).
In 11 there are 55 fifths (11 × 5).

14) 12
There are 18 posts, so $\frac{1}{3}$ of 18 is 18 ÷ 3 = 6.
So 6 posts are painted red which means that 18 − 6 = 12 posts are not painted red.

15) $\frac{4}{9}$
50 + 40 = 90. So $\frac{40}{90}$ of the members were men. This can be simplified to $\frac{4}{9}$ if you divide the numerator and the denominator by 10.

Page 8

1) 5:7
There are 5 shaded rectangles and 7 non-shaded rectangles.

2) 7:11
There and 7 shaded parts and 11 non-shaded parts.

3) 16 hours
It takes 2 hours to paint 3 pictures.
24 is 8 times 3 (3 × 8 = 24) so it will take 8 times longer to paint 24 pictures, 2 × 8 = 16 hours.

4) 72 cars
The total number of cars would be the amount of red cars multiplied by 9 as 1 in 9 cars were red. So 8 × 9 = 72 cars.

5) 12:36
Add together the numbers in the ratio 1 + 3 = 4.
Then divide the total amount by 4 to find out how much 1 part is, 48 ÷ 4 = 12. Multiply by 3 to find out how much 3 parts are, 12 × 3 = 36. So the ratio is 12:36.

6) 40:8
Add together the numbers in the ratio 5 + 1 = 6.
Then divide the total amount by 6 to find out how much 1 part is, 48 ÷ 6 = 8. Multiply by 5 to find out how much 5 parts are, 8 × 5 = 40. So the ratio is 40:8.

7) 18:30
Add together the numbers in the ratio 3 + 5 = 8.
Then divide the total amount by 8 to find out how much 1 part is, 48 ÷ 8 = 6. Multiply by 3 to find out how much 3 parts are, 6 × 3 = 18, and multiply by 5 to work out how much 5 parts are, 6 × 5 = 30. So the ratio is 18:30.

8) 4:44
Add together the numbers in the ratio 1 + 11 = 12.
Then divide the total amount by 12 to find out how much 1 part is, 48 ÷ 12 = 4. Multiply by 11 to find out how much 11 parts are, 4 × 11 = 44. So the ratio is 4:44.

9) 32:16
Add together the numbers in the ratio 2 + 1 = 3.
Then divide the total amount by 3 to find out how much 1 part is, 48 ÷ 3 = 16. Multiply by 2 to find out how much 2 parts are, 16 × 2 = 32. So the ratio is 32:16.

10) 39:9
Add together the numbers in the ratio 13 + 3 = 16.
Then divide the total amount by 16 to find out how much 1 part is, 48 ÷ 16 = 3. Multiply by 13 to find out how much 13 parts are, 3 × 13 = 39, and multiply by 3 to work out how much 3 parts are 3 × 3 = 9. So the ratio is 39:9.

11) 24 cupcakes
900 ÷ 300 = 3 times as much butter as the recipe needs. So this amount of butter would make 3 times as many cupcakes, 8 × 3 = 24.

12) 11:16
There are 11 snakes, and 5 more lizards than snakes, so 11 + 5 = 16 lizards. The ratio of snakes to lizards is 11:16.

Answers

Page 9

1) 0.5
To convert a percentage into a decimal, divide it by 100.
50% ÷ 100 = 0.5

2) $\frac{3}{10}$
30% means '30 out of 100'. So that's $\frac{30}{100}$.
This can be simplified to $\frac{3}{10}$ by dividing the numerator and the denominator by 10.

3) 75%
To convert a decimal into a percentage, multiply it by 100.
0.75 × 100 = 75%.

4) 0.2
To convert a percentage into a decimal, divide it by 100.
20% ÷ 100 = 0.2

5) 60%
To convert a decimal into a percentage, multiply it by 100.
0.6 × 100 = 60%

6) £6
50% = $\frac{1}{2}$ of £12. 12 ÷ 2 = 6, 12 − 6 = £6.

7) £16
20% = $\frac{1}{5}$ of £20. 20 ÷ 5 = 4, 20 − 4 = £16

8) £30
25% = $\frac{1}{4}$ of £40. 40 ÷ 4 = 10, 40 − 10 = £30

9) £7.20
10% = $\frac{1}{10}$ of £8. 8 ÷ 10 = 0.8, 8 − 0.8 = £7.20.

10) £3.80
£4 = 400p. 10% of 400p = 400 ÷ 10 = 40p
5% = half of 10% of 400p = 40 ÷ 2 = 20p,
£4.00 − 20p = £3.80

11) 70%
$\frac{3}{10}$ were black which means that $\frac{7}{10}$ were brown. To find $\frac{7}{10}$ as a percentage you need to turn it into an equivalent fraction with 100 as the denominator. Multiply the numerator and the denominator by 10 to get $\frac{70}{100}$ = 70%.

12) 7.5 g
10% of 50 g would be 50 ÷ 10 = 5 g. 5% would be
5 g ÷ 2 = 2.5 g. So 15% would be 5 g + 2.5 g = 7.5 g.

13) B
Add up the other percentages in the pie chart:
40 + 35 + 15 = 90%. That means that 100% − 90% = 10% of the pupils had red hair. 10% = $\frac{10}{100}$. This can be simplified to $\frac{1}{10}$ by dividing the numerator and the denominator by 10.

14) 25% of 40
$\frac{1}{4}$ of 100. 100 ÷ 4 = 25
75% of 80. 75% is $\frac{3}{4}$, so 80 ÷ 4 = 20. 20 × 3 = 60.
50% of 60. 50% is $\frac{1}{2}$, so 60 ÷ 2 = 30
$\frac{3}{5}$ of 25. 25 ÷ 5 = 5, 5 × 3 = 15
25% of 40. 25% is $\frac{1}{4}$, so 40 ÷ 4 = 10

15) C
Go through each option and convert the fractions into decimals by first making them into fractions out of 100.
Then work out which is correct.
$\frac{1}{5}$ — multiply the numerator and the denominator by 20 to get $\frac{20}{100}$ = 0.2. 0.2 is not greater than 0.2
$\frac{1}{2}$ — multiply the numerator and the denominator by 50 to get $\frac{50}{100}$ = 0.5. 0.5 is not equal to 0.2
$\frac{1}{4}$ — multiply the numerator and the denominator by 25 to get $\frac{25}{100}$ = 0.25. 0.35 is greater than 0.25, so this is correct.

Section Two — Working with Numbers
Page 10

There are lots of different methods you can use for addition. Look at the numbers that you are adding and choose a suitable method that you feel confident with.

1) £3.50
A sandwich costs £2 and an orange juice costs £1.50.
So total cost = £2 + £1.50 = £3.50.

2) £2.75
Tea costs £1.40 and a teacake costs £1.35.
So total cost = £1.40 + £1.35. Partition £1.35 into
£1 + 35p: £1.40 + £1 = £2.40, £2.40 + 35p = £2.75.

3) £3.10
Coffee costs £1.25 and a scone costs £1.85.
So total cost = £1.25 + £1.85. Partition £1.25 into
£1 + 20p + 5p: 1.85 + £1 = £2.85, £2.85 + 20p = £3.05,
£3.05 + 5p = £3.10.

4) £3.35
Orange juice costs £1.50 and a scone costs £1.85.
So total cost = £1.50 + £1.85. Partition £1.50 into
£1 + 50p. £1.85 + £1 = £2.85, £2.85 + 50p = £3.35.

5) £3.20
A scone costs £1.85 and a teacake costs £1.35.
So total cost = £1.85 + £1.35. To get from £1.85
to £2, you need to add on 15p, so partition £1.35 into
15p + £1.20: £1.85 + 15p = £2, £2 + £1.20 = £3.20.

6) 451
Partitioning is a good method for working out 428 + 23.
Partition 23 into 20 + 3 and add each part separately:
428 + 20 = 448, 448 + 3 = 451.

7) 10.1
Partition 3.7 into 3 + 0.7 and add each part separately:
6.4 + 3 = 9.4, 9.4 + 0.7 = 10.1.

8) 24.8
Partition 8.5 into 8 and 0.5 and add each part separately:
16.3 + 8 = 24.3, 24.3 + 0.5 = 24.8.

9) 39.2
Partition 12.5 into 12 + 0.5 and add each part separately:
26.7 + 12 = 38.7, 38.7 + 0.5 = 39.2

10) 16.22
Partition 3.72 into 3 + 0.7 + 0.02 and add each part separately:
12.5 + 3 = 15.5, 15.5 + 0.7 = 16.2, 16.2 + 0.02 = 16.22.

11) 3½ (or 3.5) kg
The total weight is: 1 kg + 1½ kg + ½ kg + ½ kg.
Add on each weight separately:
1 kg + 1½ kg = 2½ kg, 2½ kg + ½ kg = 3 kg
3 kg + ½ kg = 3½ kg.

12) 447 cm
Their total height = 147 cm + 149 cm + 151 cm.
It's easiest to add 149 cm and 151 cm first because
49 cm + 51 cm = 100 cm. So 149 cm + 151 cm = 300 cm.
300 cm + 147 cm = 447 cm.

13) £1.83
Latisha has: 50p + (6 × 20p) + 5p + (4 × 2p)
= 50p + 120p + 5p + 8p = £1.70 + 5p + 8p = £1.83.

14) B
The total weight of the family is 79 kg + 55 kg + 42 kg + 37 kg.
First add the tens — 70 + 50 + 40 + 30 = 190
Then add the units — 9 + 5 + 2 + 7 = 23
Then add them together — 190 + 23 = 213 kg
213 kg is below the maximum weight of 250 kg,
so the family can sit in one log. Statement B is true.

15) 82.5 litres
31.5 litres + 20.75 litres + 30.25 litres were used.
Add the whole number parts first, then add the decimal parts:
31 + 20 + 30 = 81
0.5 + 0.75 + 0.25 = 1.5
81 + 1.5 = 82.5
So 82.5 litres were used in total.

Page 11

There are lots of different methods you can use for subtraction.
Look at the numbers that you are working with and choose
a suitable method that you feel confident with.

1) 51
Partition the 25 into 20 + 5 and subtract each part separately:
76 − 20 = 56, 56 − 5 = 51.

2) 49
18 is very close to 20, so to subtract 18 easily, subtract 20
and adjust by adding 2 (because 20 = 18 + 2).
67 − 20 = 47, 47 + 2 = 49

3) 29
To work out 112 − 83 count up from 83 to 112:
83 + 17 = 100, 100 + 12 = 112, 17 + 12 = 29.

4) 17
Partition 103 into 100 + 3 and subtract each part:
120 − 100 = 20, 20 − 3 = 17.

5) 5.7
To work out 18.3 − 12.6 count up from 12.6 to 18.3:
12.6 + 0.4 = 13
13 + 5 = 18
18 + 0.3 = 18.3
0.4 + 5 + 0.3 = 5.7.

6) £1.45
Count up from £3.55 to £5:
£3.55 + 45p = £4, £4 + £1 = £5, 45p + £1 = £1.45.

7) £4.11
Count up from 89p to £5:
89p + 11p = £1, £1 + £4 = £5, 11p + £4 = £4.11.

8) £0.63
Count up from £4.37 to £5:
£4.37 + 3p = £4.40, £4.40 + 60p = £5
3p + 60p = 63p = £0.63.

9) £2.92
Count up from £2.08 to £5:
£2.08 + 92p = £3, £3 + £2 = £5, 92p + £2 = £2.92.

10) £3.89
Count up from £1.11 to £5:
£1.11 + 89p = £2, £2 + £3 = £5, 89p + £3 = £3.89.

11) B
Sam can add 25 kg − 15.7 kg to his suitcase.
Count up from 15.7 kg to 25 kg:
15.7 kg + 0.3 kg = 16 kg
16 kg + 9 kg = 25 kg
0.3 kg + 9 kg = 9.3 kg. This is answer B.

12) 0.22
Count up from 1.78 to 2:
1.78 + 0.02 = 1.80
1.80 + 0.20 = 2
0.02 + 0.20 = 0.22.

13) £17.30
Frankie spent £1.80 + £1.25.
Partition £1.25 into £1 + 20p + 5p
and add each bit separately:
£1.80 + £1 = £2.80
£2.80 + 20p = £3
£3 + 5p = £3.05.
So the amount of money he has left is £20.35 − £3.05.
£20.35 − £3 = £17.35
£17.35 − 5p = £17.30.

14) 8 °C
Count up from −6 °C to 2 °C. There is 6 °C between −6 °C
and 0 °C, and then there is 2 °C between 0 °C and 2 °C.
So the difference between −6 °C and 2 °C is 6 °C + 2 °C = 8 °C.

15) 2.14 litres
After Daisy pours 0.56 litres of juice into the first glass,
there are 3 − 0.56 litres left in the jug. Partition 0.56
into 0.50 + 0.06 and subtract each part:
3 − 0.50 = 2.50, 2.50 − 0.06 = 2.44 litres.
After pouring 0.3 litres into the second glass there are
2.44 − 0.3 = 2.14 litres left in the jug.

Page 12

To multiply by 10, move the digits one place to the left and add
zeros in any empty places between the digits and the decimal
point. To multiply by 100, move the digits 2 places to the left,
and to multiply the digits by 1000, move the digits 3 places to
the left. To divide by 10, 100 or 1000, move the digits 1, 2 or 3
places to the right.

1) 2700		2) 3500	
3) 784		4) 655	
5) 400		6) 43	
7) 367.2		8) 50.5	
9) 2.3		10) 0.085	

11) £85
Cecil receives 100 × 85p = 8500p.
£1 = 100p, so 8500p = £8500 ÷ 100 = £85.

Answers

12) 155
The school needs 1548 ÷ 10 = 154.8 boxes of planners. They can only buy whole boxes, so round up to the nearest whole number. They need 155 boxes.

13) 130
Work backwards from Patrick's final answer (1.3). The last thing he did was divide by 1000 to get 1.3. So multiply 1.3 by 1000: 1.3 × 1000 = 1300. He multiplied his starting number by 10 to get 1300. So divide 1300 by 10: 1300 ÷ 10 = 130. Patrick's starting number was 130.

14) 1.25
1250 ÷ 1000 = 1.25, so the missing number is 1.25.

15) D
First work out the right hand side of the equation: 0.1283 × 100 = 12.83
So 1283 _____ = 12.83
12.83 × 100 = 1283, so 1283 ÷ 100 = 12.83.
So the missing expression is ÷ 100. This is answer D.

Pages 13-14

To multiply a number by 12, partition 12 into 10 + 2. Then multiply the number by 10 and then by 2, then add the two products together.

1) 108
9 × 10 = 90, 9 × 2 = 18, 90 + 18 = 108.

2) 144
12 × 10 = 120, 12 × 2 = 24, 120 + 24 = 144.

3) 180
15 × 10 = 150, 15 × 2 = 30, 150 + 30 = 180.

4) 240
2 × 12 = 24. 20 is ten times larger than 2, so 20 × 12 = 240.

5) 4800
4 × 12 = 48, 400 is 100 times larger than 4, so 400 × 12 = 4800.

6) 180
Partition 36 into 30 + 6, and multiply 5 by each of these parts: 30 × 5 = 150, 6 × 5 = 30, 150 + 30 = 180.

7) 76
Partition 19 into 10 + 9, and multiply 4 by each of these parts: 10 × 4 = 40, 9 × 4 = 36, 40 + 36 = 76.
Alternatively, 19 is 1 less than 20.
So 19 × 4 = (20 × 4) − (1 × 4) = 80 − 4 = 76.

8) 4.5
Partition 1.5 into 1 + 0.5, and multiply 3 by each of these parts:
1 × 3 = 3, 0.5 × 3 = 1.5, 3 + 1.5 = 4.5.

9) 21
Partition 3.5 into 3 + 0.5, and multiply 6 by each of these parts:
3 × 6 = 18
0.5 × 6 = 3
18 + 3 = 21.

10) 9
Partition 2.25 into 2 + 0.25, and multiply 4 by each of these parts:
2 × 4 = 8, 0.25 × 4 = 1, 8 + 1 = 9.

11) £1.45
The total cost = 5 × 29p. 29p = 30p − 1p, so one way of working this out is to do 5 × 30p = 150p then subtract the extra 5 × 1p = 5p you added. 150p − 5p = 145p = £1.45

12) £2.35
3 packets of crisps cost 45p × 3 = (40p × 3) + (5p × 3)
= 120p + 15p = 135p = £1.35. 4 toffee crunches cost
25p × 4 = £1. So total cost = £1.35 + £1 = £2.35.

13) 720 ml
6 × 120 ml of water must be added. Partition 120 ml into 100 ml + 20 ml and multiply each part by 6:
6 × 100 ml = 600 ml
6 × 20 ml = 120 ml
600 ml + 120 ml = 720 ml.

14) D
The answer choices are all very different, so use rounding to find the correct one. 12.6 rounds to 13, and 5.5 rounds to 6. 13 × 6 = (10 × 6) + (3 × 6) = 60 + 18 = 78. The only answer choice that is reasonably close to 78 is D, 69.3.

15) A
There are 6 lots of 420 added together, so this is 6 × 420.
6 × 420 = 12 × _____ As 6 is half of 12, the missing number must be half of 420 in order for both sides of the equation to stay the same. 420 ÷ 2 = 210.

16) 2
0.008 = 8 ÷ 1000. So 250 × 0.008 is the same as (250 × 8) ÷ 1000. You're told that 250 × 8 = 2000, so 250 × 0.008 = 2000 ÷ 1000 = 2.

17) D
462 is double 231, so 75 × 462 will be double 75 × 231.
75 × 231 = 17 325, so 75 × 462 = 2 × 17 325
Work this out by partitioning 17 325 into 17 000 + 300 + 25 and multiplying each part by 2:
2 × 17 000 = 34 000
2 × 300 = 600
2 × 25 = 50.
34 000 + 600 + 50 = 34 650.
Alternatively, you could notice that 17 325 ends in 25 and 25 × 2 = 50. So if you multiply 17 325 by 2, the number must end in 50. The only option that ends in 50 is D.

18) £54
There are 12 months in a year, so Sarah spends 12 × £1.50 each year on comics. 12 × £1.50 = (12 × £1) + (12 × 50p) = £12 + £6 = £18. Over three years she spends
3 × £18 = (3 × £10) + (3 × £8) = £30 + £24 = £54.

19) £66
The cost of hiring one bike for four hours is
£5.50 × 4 = (£5 × 4) + (50p × 4) = £20 + £2 = £22.
The cost of hiring three bikes for four hours is £22 × 3 = £66.

20) C
43 is 4.3 × 10, and 0.38 = 3.8 ÷ 10. The × 10 and the ÷ 10 cancel each other out, so 43 × 0.38 is the same as 4.3 × 3.8, which equals 16.34 (C).

21) D
98p = £1 − 2p, so the cost of 26 pens can be written as:
26 × 98p = (26 × £1) − (26 × 2p) = (26 × £1) − 52p.
The cost of a ruler is £1.49 = £1.50 − 1p, so the total cost of 11 rulers can be written as:
11 × £1.49 = (11 × £1.50) − (11 × 1p) = (11 × £1.50) − 11p
So the total cost = 26 × £1 − 52p + 11 × £1.50 − 11p

22) 0.56
7 × 8 = 56, 0.7 = 7 ÷ 10 and 0.8 = 8 ÷ 10
So 0.7 × 0.8 = 56 ÷ 10 ÷ 10 = 0.56.

23) C
You're told that 2025 = 45 × 45. 4050 is double 2025, so you need to double one of the 45s in the multiplication to get the answer 4050. 45 × 2 = 90. So 90 × 45 = 4050.

24) 48
First find out how many packs Mr Lewis can buy with £10. A good way of doing this is to estimate the answer using an easy multiplication fact, and then adjust.
10 × 80p = £8
11 × 80p = £8.80
12 × 80p = £9.60 (this is only 40p less than £10, so is the most he can buy). So Mr Lewis buys 12 packs of 4 rolls. This is 12 × 4 = 48 rolls altogether.

Page 15

1) 6
8 × 6 = 48, so 48 ÷ 8 = 6.

2) 8
7 × 8 = 56, so 56 ÷ 7 = 8.

3) 8
9 × 8 = 72, so 72 ÷ 9 = 8.

4) 11
Split 66 up into 60 + 6 and divide each number separately.
60 ÷ 6 = 10, 6 ÷ 6 = 1, 10 + 1 = 11

5) 17
Split 51 up into 30 + 21 and divide each number separately.
30 ÷ 3 = 10, 21 ÷ 3 = 7, 10 + 7 = 17

6) £20
£60 ÷ 3 = £20

7) £15
Split £45 up into £30 + £15 and divide each number separately.
£30 ÷ 3 = £10, £15 ÷ 3 = £5, £10 + £5 = £15

8) £33
Split £99 up into £90 + £9 and divide each number separately.
£90 ÷ 3 = £30, £9 ÷ 3 = £3, £30 + £3 = £33

9) £3.33
Split £9.99 up into £9 + 90p + 9p and divide each number separately.
£9 ÷ 3 = £3, 90p ÷ 3 = 30p, 9p ÷ 3 = 3p
£3 + 30p + 3p = £3.33

10) £3.50
Split £10.50 up into £9 + £1.50 and divide each number separately.
£9 ÷ 3 = £3, £1.50 ÷ 3 = 50p, £3 + 50p = £3.50

11) 7
The number of boxes needed is: 40 ÷ 6 = 6 r 4 (because 6 × 6 = 36, and 40 − 36 = 4).
You need to round 6 r 4 up to 7 boxes to fit all 40 eggs in (there will be 2 spaces left over).

12) £18
£72 = £40 + £32, £40 ÷ 4 = £10, £32 ÷ 4 = £8
£10 + £8 = £18.

13) A
There can't be 7 biscuits left over, or each dog could have one more biscuit.

14) 17
To find the number of rolls needed, divide 132 m by 8 m:

```
    0  1  6  remainder 4
8 ) 1 ¹3 ⁵2
```

To get the number of rolls needed, round 16 remainder 4 up to 17. (16 rolls won't be enough.)

15) 40
The number of 40 g slices is 1600 g ÷ 40 g.

```
        4  0
40 ) 1 ¹6¹6 0  0
```

So there are 40 slices.

Page 16

1) 52
56 − 4 = 52

2) 77
73 + 4 = 77

3) 24
6 × 4 = 24

4) 8
32 ÷ 4 = 8

5) 10
3 × 4 = 12
12 − 2 = 10
To find a term in the sequence, you swap n in $3n - 1$ for the term number and work out the value.

6) 2
For the 1st term, n = 1. 3 × 1 − 1 = 2.

7) 17
For the 6th term, n = 6. 3 × 6 − 1 = 17.

8) 29
For the 10th term, n = 10. 3 × 10 − 1 = 29.

9) 44
For the 15th term, n = 15. 3 × 15 − 1 = 44.

10) 59
For the 20th term, n = 20. 3 × 20 − 1 = 59.

11) £60
To find the cost for 5 hours, swap z in $25 + 7z$ for 5 and work out the value. 25 + 7 × 5 = 25 + 35 = 60.
(Remember to do the multiplication before the addition.)
So the cost is £60.

12) £175
To find the cost of 20 kits, swap y in $15 + 8y$ for 20 and work out the value. 15 + 8 × 20 = 15 + 160 = 175.
(Remember to do the multiplication before the addition again.)
So the cost is £175.

Answers

13) B
Gaby is x years old and her mum is 24 years older.
So her mum is $x + 24$ years old.

14) E
The books are £3 each, so y books cost £3 × y, or £3y.
There is one lot of postage at £4.99 to add on,
so the total cost in pounds is $3y + 4.99$.

Section Three —
Number Problems
Page 17

BODMAS tells you that you need to work out the part of a calculation in brackets first. Then use this value to do the second part of the calculation.

1) 150
37 + 13 = 50
50 × 3 = 150

2) 68
29 − 17 = 12
56 + 12 = 68

3) 5
18 + 12 = 30
150 ÷ 30 = 5

4) 214
3 × 7 = 21
235 − 21 = 214

5) £8.75
Entry for two children costs 2 × £3.25 = £6.50.
Entry for one toddler costs £2.25. £6.50 + £2.25 = £8.75.

6) E
The cost of entry for three 14 year olds is 3 × £3.25.
The cost of three Go Kart rides is 3 × £1.50.
So the total cost is 3 × 3.25 + 3 × 1.50. This is answer E.

7) £8.50
The cost of entry for two children is £3.25 × 2 = £6.50.
The cost of two Go Kart rides is £1.50 × 2 = £3.
The cost of two Snack Packs is £1 × 2 = £2.
The total cost is £6.50 + £3 + £2 = £11.50.
From a £20 note, David would receive £20 − £11.50 = £8.50 in change.

8) 36 500
BODMAS tells you that you need to do the multiplications first so you need to find (79 × 365) + (365 × 21).
79 lots of 365 and 21 lots of 35 is the same as
79 + 21 = 100 lots of 365. 100 × 365 = 36 500.

9) D
BODMAS tells you that you need to work out multiplications first, then additions, then subtractions. Option D is the only option that doesn't equal 81. 50 × 10 = 500, 500 + 39 = 539, 539 − 8 = 531

10) 8
BODMAS tells you that you need to work out multiplication first, then do the subtraction.
2.5 × 8 = 20, 20 − 12 = 8.

11) A
Find the options with the biggest multiplication and work them out.
10 × 9 is the biggest multiplication, so
A: 10 × 9 = 90, 90 + 8 = 98, 98 − 7 = 91.
C: 9 × 10 = 90, 90 + 7 = 97, 97 − 8 = 89.
So A is the answer.

12) 375 g
12 × 1.5 = 18, so Max needs to use 1.5 times as much sugar to make 18 fairy cakes. 1.5 × 250 = 250 + 125 = 375 g, so he needs 375 g of sugar.

Pages 18-19

1) 50p
Subtract the cost of the banana from £2.30 to find the cost of the three mangos: £2.30 − 80p = £1.50. Divide the cost of the three mangos by 3 to find the cost of one mango: £1.50 ÷ 3 = 50p.

2) £75
She kept 2 of the 5 pairs so she returned 5 − 2 = 3 pairs. Each pair costs £25, so she will be refunded 3 × £25 = £75 by the shop.

3) 50
Arya buys 4 × 250 g = 1000 g of food in total. The gerbil eats 20 g of food each day so it'll take 5 days to eat 100 g (5 × 20 = 100). 1000 is ten times larger than 100, so the food will last for 5 × 10 = 50 days.

4) £28.37
Mrs Cooper pays 2 × £20 = £40 in total. She is given £11.63 in change, so the cost of the fuel is £40.00 − £11.63 = £28.37.

5) D
Add together the items in each option to find the option that adds up to £1.60. In option D, 1 pencil + 1 rubber + 1 pen is 55p + 35p + 70p = £1.60.

6) E
$\frac{4}{12}$ of the apple cake was sold and $\frac{4}{6}$ of the carrot cake was sold. $\frac{4}{6}$ is the same as $\frac{8}{12}$. So in total $\frac{4}{12} + \frac{8}{12} = \frac{12}{12}$ was sold, which is the same as 1 whole cake.

7) B
The shop sells one kilogram of potatoes for £1.20, so in total they make 20 × £1.20 = £24. They spent £15 buying the potatoes, so the difference between what they spent and what they earned is £24 − £15 = £9.

8) 5
Zac and Isa are making 13 bags so they need 13 × 3 = 39 toys in total. In 4 packs of toys there will be 4 × 9 = 36 toys which isn't enough. In 5 packs of toys there will be 5 × 9 = 45 toys which is enough. So they need to buy 5 packs of toys.

9) A
Double the sale price of the jacket until you reach £148. Each time you double the price is 1 week in the sale.
£18.50 × 2 = £37, £37 × 2 = £74, £74 × 2 = £148.
The jacket has been in the sale for 3 weeks.

10) £15.75
The cost of the beads needed to make each bracelet is 45p × 10 = £4.50. The cost of the wire strip is 75p, so the cost of making each bracelet is £4.50 + 75p = £5.25.
So the cost of making 3 bracelets is £5.25 × 3 = £15.75.

11) £6.50
There are 10 mm in 1 cm, so the tower is 13 × 10 = 130 mm high. Each coin is 2 mm thick, so there are 130 ÷ 2 = 65 coins in the tower. The value of 65 ten pence coins is 65 × 10 = 650p. 650p = £6.50.

12) £4.56
Add up the cost of each item on the menu to find the total cost: £1.75 + £3.25 = £5.00, £5.00 + £3.45 = £8.45, £8.45 + £1.99 = £10.44. The amount of change Oliver will receive is £15 − £10.44 = £4.56.

13) D
To find the minimum number of songs that can fit on the MP3 player, you need to imagine that each song is the longest time possible — 3 minutes. 45 ÷ 3 = 15, so 15 songs is the minimum number that Grace can store.

14) 3
Work backwards through the calculation from 51 to find Ant's starting number. The last thing he did was to add 15, so subtract 15: 51 − 15 = 36. He multiplied a number by itself to give 36, so find this number. 6 × 6 = 36, so the number Ant multiplied by itself was 6. He doubled the number to get 6, so halve 6 to find the starting number: 6 ÷ 2 = 3.

15) 42p
In the pack of 4 peppers, the cost per pepper is £1.80 ÷ 4 = 45p. In the pack of 6 peppers, the cost per pepper is £2.52 ÷ 6. Work this out using short division:

$$6 \overline{)2.2^25^12}$$
$$= 0.42$$

So the cheapest amount you could pay per pepper is £0.42 = 42p.

16) D
A: This can be true, e.g. there could be 30 tulips and 25 daffodils.
B: This can be true, e.g. there could be 34 daffodils and 21 tulips.
C: This can be true, e.g. there could be 28 daffodils and 27 tulips.
D: This cannot be true. The total number of bulbs is odd (55), so the sum of the number of daffodils and tulips must be an odd number added to an even number. The difference between an odd number and an even number is always odd. 8 is an even number, so this cannot be true.
E: This can be true, e.g. there could be 30 tulips and 25 daffodils.

17) £8.20
Each person is having one cupcake so Laura needs 20 cupcakes. This will cost 20 × 15p = 300p. 300p = £3.
Each person is having half of a doughnut so Laura needs 20 ÷ 2 = 10 doughnuts. This costs 10 × 52p = 520p. 520p = £5.20. So, altogether Laura will spend £3 + £5.20 = £8.20 on the cakes.

Section Four — Data Handling
Page 20

1) Nina
The highest score in the table is 43. Nina got 43, so Nina scored the highest mark.

2) 24
Nina scored 43 and Paula scored 19. So the difference between their marks is 43 − 19 = 24.

3) Paula
Kate scored 39, so a score exactly 20 less than this would be 39 − 20 = 19. Paula scored 19.

4) 13
The test was out of 50 and George scored 37. So George must have lost 50 − 37 = 13 marks.

5) Train C
Counting from the departure time to the arrival time tells you how long each train takes. There are 2 hours from 12.00 to 14:00, and a further 45 minutes to 14.45. So train C takes 2 hours 45 minutes.

6) Train B
10:30 to 11:30 is 1 hour, plus 30 minutes to get to 12:00. So train B takes 1 hour 30 minutes.

7) Train B
Train B arrives in Banbridge at 12:00. The next train (Train C) doesn't arrive until 14:45. This would be too late if Robert needs to be in Banbridge by 12:15.

8) Alan
The faster the runner the lower their time. Ahmed had the fastest time at 10.9 s, followed by Louisa with 11.1 s and then Alan with 12.8 s, so Alan came third.

9) A
Archers who scored 16-20 points or 21-25 points scored more than 15 points in total. 13 archers scored 16-20 points and 5 archers scored 21-25 points, so 13 + 5 = 18 scored more than 15 — so A is true.

10) 2
From the table, Kylie spent £11.50 on cakes in total. She spent £1.50 on a Victoria sponge and £4.00 on lemon drizzles, so she must have spent £11.50 − £4.00 − £1.50 = £6.00 on fruit cakes. Fruit cakes cost £3.00 each, so she must have ordered 6.00 ÷ 3.00 = 2 fruit cakes in total.

Pages 21-22

1) P4
The class with the fewest children will have the lowest bar — class P4.

2) 25
Each division on the vertical axis shows 2 children. The top of the bar for class P2 is $2\frac{1}{2}$ divisions above 20. $2\frac{1}{2}$ divisions is the same as 5 children (2 × $2\frac{1}{2}$ = 5). Class P2 has 20 + 5 = 25 children.

3) P1 and P5
Find the point on the vertical axis that shows 28 children, then look across to see which bars are taller than this point. P1 and P5 are the only classes with more than 28 children.

4) 7
Reading from the bar chart, class P3 has 28 children in it. Class P4 only has 21 children in it. So there are 28 − 21 = 7 more children in class P3 than in P4.

5) 14 °C
Find 11:00 on the horizontal axis and move straight up until you reach the graph line. At this point, move across to the vertical axis and read off the temperature (14 °C).

6) 5 °C
The lowest temperature will be the lowest point on the graph. The lowest temperature was recorded at 9:00. Reading off the graph, the temperature at 9:00 was 5 °C.

7) B
The biggest temperature rise happens between the two times on the graph that have the biggest vertical difference between them. This happens between 10:00 and 11:00 when the rise in temperature is 14 − 8 = 6 °C.

8) 11
Each symbol on the pictogram shows 2 people.
There are 5½ symbols for tea.
5 × 2 = 10 and ½ × 2 = 1
10 + 1 = 11 people prefer tea.

9) C
Read off the graph how many tourists chose each city:
London = 30, Bristol = 16, Manchester = 24, Liverpool = 13, York = 19. Then find the total number of people in the survey by adding all these values together.
30 + 16 + 24 + 13 + 19 = 102.

10) 28 m
Reading off the graph, 1 floor is 2 m tall, so 14 floors would be 2 × 14 = 28 m tall. Alternatively, reading off the graph, 7 floors are 14 m tall. 14 ÷ 7 = 2, so 14 floors must be 2 × 14 = 28 m tall.

11) 4 hours
Find the total hours Sam and Sanjay worked out by adding together the number of hours they worked out each week.
Sam worked out for 4 + 8 + 10 = 22 hours.
Sanjay worked out for 5 + 4 + 9 = 18 hours.
22 − 18 = 4 so Sam worked out for 4 hours more than Sanjay.

12) B
Each school played 32 matches. From the pie charts, Eastwick School drew half of their matches.
32 ÷ 2 = 16, so Eastwick School played 16 drawn matches and statement B is true.

13) 9
Each symbol on the pictogram shows 4 CDs. So each ½ symbol shows 2 CDs, and each ¼ symbol shows 1 CD.
The Victories sold 4½ symbols = 4 × 4 CDs + 2 CDs = 18 CDs.
The Moofs sold 2¼ symbols = 2 × 4 CDs + 1 CD = 9 CDs.
18 − 9 = 9, so the Victories sold 9 more CDs than the Moofs.

14) 40
2 bedroom and 3 bedroom houses make up all the houses with more than one bedroom. The right angle signs in the sections for 2 bedroom and 3 bedroom houses mean that they each take up ¼ of the pie chart. You can work that out because there are 4 right angles in a circle, so 1 right angle would be ¼ of a circle. This means that 2 and 3 bedroom houses take up ¼ + ¼ = ½ of the pie chart, so half of the people live in a house with more than 1 bedroom. The total number of people is 80, so 80 ÷ 2 = 40 people live in houses with more than 1 bedroom.

Page 23

1) 6
4 + 3 + 7 + 8 + 8 = 30. There are 5 numbers in total.
So the mean is 30 ÷ 5 = 6.

2) 9
8 + 12 + 8 + 7 + 10 = 45. There are 5 numbers in total.
So the mean is 45 ÷ 5 = 9.

3) 8
5 + 9 + 7 + 6 + 4 + 17 = 48. There are 6 numbers in total.
So the mean is 48 ÷ 6 = 8.

4) 10
9 + 8 + 10 + 12 + 9 + 12 = 60. There are 6 numbers in total.
So the mean is 60 ÷ 6 = 10.

5) 8
10 + 8 + 11 + 11 + 2 + 4 + 12 + 6 = 64.
There are 8 numbers in total. So the mean is 64 ÷ 8 = 8.

6) 14 s
When the five sprint times are added together you get:
14 + 12 + 15 + 17 + 12 = 70. There are 5 times in total.
So the mean time is 70 ÷ 5 = 14.

7) 11
2 + 3 + 9 + 10 + 12 + 3 + 5 + 7 + 19 + 20 + 31 = 121.
There are 11 scores in total.
So the mean score is 121 ÷ 11 = 11.

8) 12 mm
9 + 12 + 14 + 13 = 48. There are 4 numbers in total.
So the mean is 48 ÷ 4 = 12.

9) 21
30 + 6 + 9 + 10 + 11 + 60 = 126.
There are 6 scores in total.
So the mean score is 126 ÷ 6 = 21.

10) E
The mean of E is (16 + 4 + 9 + 7 + 14) ÷ 5 = 50 ÷ 5 = 10.
So E is the correct answer.

Section Five — Shape and Space
Page 24

1) A
Small squares are used to show right angles, so A is definitely a right angle.

2) C
Angle C is biggest because it is the only angle that is bigger than 180°.

3) B and E
An acute angle is smaller than a right angle.

4) D
An obtuse angle is bigger than a right angle but smaller than two right angles (the angle along a straight line).

5) C
Reflex angles are larger than two right angles (the angle along a straight line).

6) B
A right angle is 90°, so 45° is half a right angle.
Angle B is about half a right angle.

7) A
A right angle is 90°, so 180° is two right angles, or the angle along a straight line. Angle A is along a straight line.

8) E
135° is bigger than a right angle (90°) but smaller than the angle along a straight line (180°). So angle E is the only one that could be 135°.

9) D
70° is slightly smaller than a right angle (90°).
C is the only angle that is slightly smaller than a right angle.

10) C
A right angle is like the corner of a square.
Angle C looks like it is this size.

11) 2
The right angles that the ant turns
through are marked on this diagram:

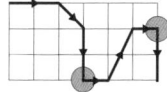

12) 270°
Turning clockwise from facing north to facing west means
turning through three right angles. This is 3 × 90° = 270°.

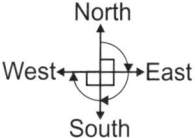

13) 120°
The angle between the hands is equal to 1 right angle (90°) plus
one-third of a right angle (90° ÷ 3 = 30°). So the total angle is
90° + 30° = 120°.
Alternatively, just by looking at the angle you can see that it is
between 90° and 180°. The only options between these angles
are 120° and 150°. You can tell from the diagram that the angle
is closer to 90° than 180°, so the answer must be 120°.

14) 110°
There are 180° on a straight line,
so angle y = 180° − 40° − 30° = 110°.

Pages 25-26

1) B
B has three sides and no right angles.

2) C
All four of the angles in C are right angles.

3) D
D has exactly one right angle.

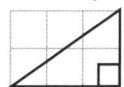

4) A
Both pairs of opposite sides in A are parallel.
There are no right angles.

5) E
E has exactly one obtuse angle (an angle that's bigger than
a right angle, but smaller than two right angles).

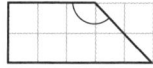

6) False
Line M is vertical, Line L isn't, so they're not parallel.

7) True
Line N is horizontal (it goes directly across the page).

8) False
Line L is not vertical. It doesn't go up the page.

9) True
Line L and Line O are at the same angle, so they are parallel.

10) True
Line M and Line N are at right angles to each other,
so they are perpendicular.

11) hexagon
The shape has 6 sides, so it is a hexagon.

12) D
Shape D goes in the shaded part of the diagram
because it is irregular (not all the sides and angles
are the same), and it has less than five sides.

13) C
The largest two shapes have 8 sides each, so they are octagons.
There are three shapes with five sides each (two are regular
pentagons and the other is an irregular pentagon). Finally,
there is one four-sided shape, which is a quadrilateral.

14) E
Pentagons don't fit together without leaving any gaps.

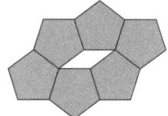

15) isosceles triangle
All triangles have three sides, and isosceles triangles
have two equal angles (and two equal sides).

16) parallelogram
The first question Maryam answers yes to is "Does it have four straight
sides?". The only shapes on the list that have four sides are a kite
and a parallelogram. The second question Maryam answers yes to
is "Are the opposite sides parallel?". The opposite sides are parallel
in a parallelogram, but not in a kite, so parallelogram is the answer.

17) kite
A kite has two pairs of equal length sides,
which are not usually parallel. The diagonals
always cross at right angles.

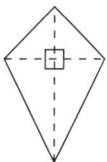

18) B
An equilateral triangle has three angles of 60° each. These are
smaller than right angles (90°), so they are acute angles.

19) D
Shape D does have a pair of parallel sides, but it also has at least
one right angle and is a quadrilateral (it has four sides).
Therefore, it belongs in all of the circles, so it should be in
the centre of the diagram where the circles all overlap.

20) 40°
The angles in a quadrilateral add up to 360°.
So: p = 360° − 100° − 100° − 120° = 40°.

Pages 27-28

1) 8 cm
Shape A is a square with sides 2 cm long.
So its perimeter is 4 × 2 cm = 8 cm.

2) 6 cm²
You can find the area of shape B by counting the squares inside it — there are 6 of them, so the area is 6 cm² (each 1 cm by 1 cm grid square has an area of 1 cm²). Alternatively, shape B is a rectangle so you can find its area by multiplying its length by its width: 3 cm × 2 cm = 6 cm².

3) 3 cm²
Find the area of shape C by counting the squares inside it — there are 3 of them, so the area is 3 cm².

4) 5 cm²
There are 4 whole squares and 2 half squares in shape D. The 2 half squares add together to make 1 whole square. So the area is 4 cm² + 1 cm² = 5 cm².

5) 8 cm
Count the number of grid square edges around the outside of shape C. There are 8, so the perimeter is 8 cm.

6) 16 cm
P is a square, so it has four sides of 4 cm.
Its perimeter is 4 × 4 cm = 16 cm.

7) 26 cm
Q is a rectangle, so it has two sides of 8 cm and two sides of 5 cm. So its perimeter is 8 cm + 8 cm + 5 cm + 5 cm = 26 cm.

8) 16 cm²
P is a square, so you can find the area by multiplying the length by the width. These are both 4 cm, so the area = 4 cm × 4 cm = 16 cm².

9) 40 cm²
P is a rectangle, so you can find the area by multiplying the length (8 cm) by the width (5 cm).
So area = 8 cm × 5 cm = 40 cm².

10) 42 cm
Shape R is a regular polygon, so all six of its sides must be 7 cm. Perimeter = 6 × 7 cm = 42 cm.

11) E
The letter P contains 8 whole squares and two half squares. As each square is 1 cm², its area is definitely more than 7 cm².

12) 1 and 2
Imagine horizontal and vertical lines drawn between the dots to form squares, then count the squares inside each shape. Shapes 1 and 2 both have areas of 4 square units.

13) m²
Metres would be the most suitable unit to measure the length and width of a tennis court, so the most suitable unit for measuring its area is m².

14) 200 cm
The middle shape is formed from 10 table mat edges. Each edge is 20 cm long, so the total perimeter of the hole is 20 × 10 = 200 cm.

15) B
Count how many grid squares are completely shaded and how many are roughly half shaded. Ignore any squares that only have a tiny amount of shading:

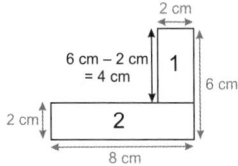

So the approximate number of squares shaded
= (6 × 1) + (8 × ½) = 6 + 4 = 10. As each square is 1 km², the area of the island is approximately 10 km².

16) 12 m
The swimming pool is a rectangle so its area is length × width: length × 6 m = 72 m², length = 72 m² ÷ 6 m = 12 m.

17) 24 cm²
Split this shape into two rectangles and work out the area of each of them. You have to work out the length of one of the sides using subtraction. Here is one way of splitting the shape up:

Area of rectangle 1 is 4 cm × 2 cm = 8 cm².
Area of rectangle 2 is 2 cm × 8 cm = 16 cm².
Total area = 8 cm² + 16 cm² = 24 cm².

18) 500 m²
First work out the area of the lawn before the garage was built:
15 m × 40 m = 600 m².
(One way of working 15 × 40 out is to partition 15 into 10 + 5 and do (10 × 40) + (5 × 40) = 400 + 200 = 600.)
Then work out the area taken up by the garage:
10 m × 10 m = 100 m².
Finally, subtract the area of the garage from the original area of the lawn: 600 m² − 100 m² = 500 m².

19) 96 cm²
Cubes have 6 identical square faces. The area of each face of this cube is 4 cm × 4 cm = 16 cm².
So the area of all 6 faces = 6 × 16 cm².
Work this out by partitioning 16 cm² into 10 cm² + 6 cm², and multiplying each part by 6: (6 × 10 cm²) + (6 × 6 cm²)
= 60 cm² + 36 cm² = 96 cm².

20) 10 cm
The notepad is a rectangle, so its perimeter is:
length + length + width + width. So:
50 cm = 15 cm + 15 cm + width + width.
50 cm = 30 cm + width + width
width + width = 50 cm − 30 cm
width + width = 20 cm
10 cm + 10 cm = 20 cm, so width = 10 cm.

21) 380 m
First find the perimeter of the garden by adding the side lengths:
20 m + 14 m + 8 m + 15 m + 5 m = 62 m.
Abdul walks this distance ten times, so he walks
62 × 10 = 620 m in total. 1 km = 1000 m, so Abdul walks 1000 m − 620 m = 380 m less than 1 km.

Page 29

1) **A and D**

2) **X**

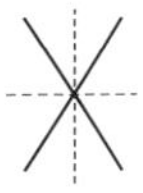

3) **F and L**
These letters have no lines of symmetry.

4) **3**

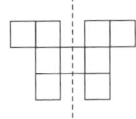

5) **1**

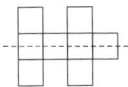

6) **square**
The shape has four sides of equal lengths and four right angles, so it is a square:

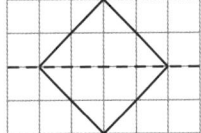

7) **C**
Shape C is a reflection of shape P (the mirror line would be vertical).

8) **3**
Square 3 must be shaded to make a symmetrical pattern.

9) **3**
This shape has 3 lines of symmetry as shown below.

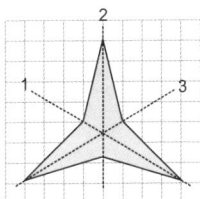

10) **E**

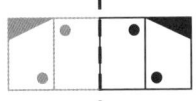

Pages 30-31

1) **C**
C is a triangular prism, it has a triangular face at each end and three rectangles connecting them.

2) **B**
B is a cone. It has a circular base and one other curved face.

3) **D**
D is a cuboid. It has 6 rectangular faces.

4) **E**
E is a square-based pyramid. Its base is a square and it has four triangular faces which meet at a point.

5) **A**
A is a triangular-based pyramid. It has four triangular faces.

6) **E**
Vertices are corners. E (square-based pyramid) has 5 corners.

7) **D**
D is a cuboid. It has four edges around the bottom, four edges around the top and four connecting the top and bottom.

8) **B**
B is a cone. It has one circular edge and one vertex (corner).

9) **A and E**
A and E are pyramids (one is triangular-based and one is square-based).

10) **C and D**
Prisms have the same shape at the top and the bottom and this shape runs all the way through them. C has a triangle running through it, and D has a rectangle.

11) **cylinder**
Cylinders have a circle at the top and a circle at the bottom, and a curved face connecting them.

12) **3 and 4**
When you are trying to decide if a net folds up into a cube, pick a central square to be the base and imagine the other squares folding up to make the sides and the top.

13) **C**
Prisms have the same shape at the top and the bottom. E.g. a triangular prism has a triangular face at the top and the bottom:

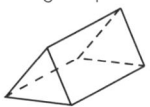

A cone has a circular face at its base and a curved face which forms a point.

A cone doesn't have the same shape at the top and the bottom so it is not a type of prism.

14) **18 cm³**
The cuboid has 3 layers, each containing 6 cubes. So there are 3 × 6 = 18 cubes in total. Each cube is 1 cm³, so the volume of the cuboid is 18 cm³. Alternatively, the volume of a cuboid is length × width × height, so volume = 3 cm × 2 cm × 3 cm = 18 cm³.

15) **A**
Trace back from the shaded box of the sorting diagram to find clues to the shape. Yes was answered to "Does the shape have two flat faces?" and to "Does the shape have a curved face?". The only shape listed that it could be is a cylinder.

16) **72**
6 cubes will fit along the 6 cm length of the box and 4 cubes will fit along the 4 cm width of the box. So on the bottom layer 6 × 4 = 24 cubes will fit. The box is 3 cm high, so 3 layers of cubes will fit. This is a total of 24 × 3 = 72 cubes.

17) D
The square will form the base of the pyramid, and the triangles will fold up around it.

18) 4
Imagine that the square labelled 5 is the base of the dice. The side labelled X will be opposite to the side labelled 3. Opposite faces add up to 7, so 3 + X = 7, meaning X = 4.

19) 3
The parallel edges are marked below:

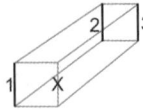

20) B
The triangles must meet together when the net folds up into a cube.

21) 11 cm
For a cuboid: volume = length × width × height.
88 cm^3 = 4 cm × 2 cm × height
88 cm^3 = 8 cm × height
So height = 88 cm^3 ÷ 8 cm = 11 cm.

Page 32

1) E   2) B   3) D

4) A

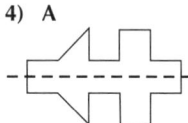

5) C and E

6) 3
Face 3 will be the base of the box and the other faces will form the sides.

7) 2 and 4
The angles and side lengths all match in these two shapes. One is just a rotation of the other..

8) D
Imagine rotating the shape 90° anti-clockwise so that it forms a backwards L-shape. The circles will then be on the very top of the shape and on the top of the "foot" of the L.
This won't change when the L is turned around to form the final L-shape shown. Option D has the circles on the very top and on the top of the "foot" of the L.

9) C
Shape F contains 12 squares, so if it is divided into four identical shapes, they will all contain 12 ÷ 4 = 3 squares.
This means only B and C are possible answers.
C can fit into shape F four times.

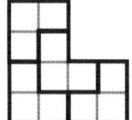

Pages 33-34

In coordinates, the horizontal (x-axis) value is always given first, then the vertical (y-axis) value.

1) (2, 2)   2) (7, 3)
3) (8, 6)   4) (5, 7)
5) (1, 8)   6) A
7) D   8) E
9) C   10) B

11) (1, 2)
Jack's route is shown on the right. The compass shows that west is left and south is downwards. He ends up at point (1, 2).

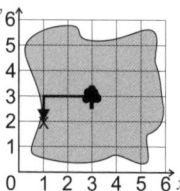

12) (4, 7)
Point Q is at (1, 2). If the shape is translated three squares to the right, this will need to be added to the x-coordinate. 1 + 3 = 4. To get the new y-coordinate, add 5 to the original y-coordinate because the shape is translated 5 squares up. 2 + 5 = 7.
So the new coordinates of point Q are (4, 7).

13) (6, 2)
The new point A will be the same perpendicular distance from the mirror line as the old point A was. It is now at (6, 2).

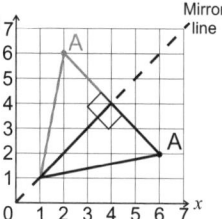

14) (3, 4)
The opposite sides of a rectangle are always the same length. So the coordinates of the rectangle's fourth corner must be at (3, 4).

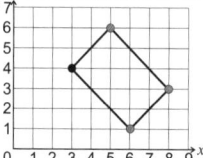

15) (5, 2)
The line is horizontal, so all the points on it must have the same y-coordinate (the second one of the pair). Therefore, the midpoint has a y-coordinate of 2. Next find the length of the line by subtracting the smaller x-coordinate from the larger one. So it's 7 − 3 = 4 units long. This means that the midpoint of the line is 4 ÷ 2 = 2 units along the line. So the x-coordinate will be 3 + 2 = 5. Therefore the coordinates of the midpoint will be (5, 2).

16) C
To form a kite, the fourth corner must have the same y-coordinate as the point (8, 5). The only option with a y-coordinate of 5 is the point (2, 5), so this is the only point that could complete the kite.

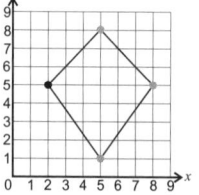

17) C
Quickly sketch a small coordinate grid and plot the points you're given. The points form a parallelogram:

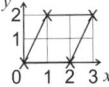

18) A
The shape is a rectangle, so corner A has the same x-coordinate as the corner at (2, 5). It has the same y-coordinate as the corner at (4,1). So, the coordinates of corner A are (2, 1).

19) (4, 5)
Between (2, 3) and (3, 4) the x-coordinate increases by 1 and the y-coordinate increases by 1. Therefore, the x-coordinate of P must be 3 + 1 = 4, and the y-coordinate must be 4 + 1 = 5.

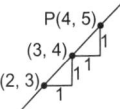

Section Six —
Units and Measures
Pages 35-36

1) kg
From the units given, g and kg can be used to measure weight. A person weighs much more than 60 g, so kg is the most likely unit to complete the sentence.

2) m
From the units given, m and km can be used to measure height. Giraffes are much less than 4.95 km tall, so m is the most likely unit to complete the sentence.

3) l
From the units given, ml and l can be used to measure the volumes of liquids. A bucket can hold much more than 18 ml, so l is the most likely unit to complete the sentence.

4) g
From the units given, g and kg can be used to measure weights. Cakes contain much less than 125 kg of sugar, so g is the most likely unit to complete the sentence.

5) km
From the units given, m and km can be used to measure heights. Mount Everest is much higher than 8.8 m, so km is the most likely unit to complete the sentence.

6) 5000 m
There are 1000 m in a km, so there are 5 × 1000 = 5000 m in 5 km.

7) 100 m
There are 1000 m in a km, so David will need to go 1000 – 900 = 100 m further to reach 1 km.

8) 79 mm
There are 10 mm in a cm, so there are 7.9 × 10 = 79 mm in 7.9 cm.

9) 500 ml
There are 1000 ml in a litre, so there are 0.5 × 1000 = 500 ml in 0.5 l.

10) 40
There are 1000 g in a kg, so James will need 1000 ÷ 25 bags to have 1 kg of sweets. 100 ÷ 25 = 4. 1000 is 10 × larger than 100, so 1000 ÷ 25 must be 10 × larger than 100 ÷ 25. 4 × 10 = 40, so James will need 40 bags of sweets.

11) B
1000 g is far too heavy for an apple. 10 g, 5 g and 1 g are all far too light for an apple. So the most likely answer is 150 g.

12) 2250 g
There are 4 divisions between 0 and 1 kg, so each division is worth 1 ÷ 4 = 0.25 kg. The arrow in the scales is pointing to one division after 2 kg, so it is pointing to 2.25 kg. There are 1000 g in a kg so weight on the scales is 2.25 × 1000 = 2250 g.

13) B
63 m is far too long for a dog, so statement B is unlikely to be true.

14) ml or cm³
The units that can be used to measure volumes of liquid are ml and l. Most people put much less than a litre of milk on their cereal, so the most sensible unit to use would be ml. Another sensible unit that can be used for measuring this amount of liquid is cm³, as 1 cm³ = 1 ml.

15) 490 g
There are 1000 g in a kg, so Anita's bar of chocolate is 0.5 × 1000 = 500 g. If she eats 10 g of it she'll have 500 – 10 = 490 g left.

16) 6
There are 1000 ml in a litre so a 1½ litre bottle of lemonade contains 1.5 × 1000 = 1500 ml. From this you could get 1500 ÷ 250 = 6 glassfuls.

17) B
There are 10 mm in a cm, so there will 150 × 10 = 1500 mm in 150 cm. So statement B is correct.

18) 4 m
8 cm on the plan is equal to 8 × 50 = 400 cm in real life. There are 100 cm in a metre, so this is equal to 400 ÷ 100 = 4 m.

19) D
There are 1000 g in a kg, so if Adam removes 50 g from the cake there will be 1000 – 50 = 950 g remaining. That's more than ¾ of the cake (which would be 750 g), so D is the correct answer.

20) 3
There are 1000 ml in a litre, so each tin holds 1 × 1000 = 1000 ml of paint. If 250 ml covers 1 m² of wall, then 1 tin of paint will cover 1000 ÷ 250 = 4 m² of wall. So to cover 12 m² of wall you'll need 12 ÷ 4 = 3 tins of paint.

21) 2 cm
There are 10 mm in a cm, so Matt has 120 ÷ 10 = 12 cm of string. There are 100 cm in a m, so Kim has 0.1 × 100 = 10 cm of string. 12 – 10 = 2, so Matt has 2 cm more string than Kim.

22) 300 g
There are 1000 g in a kg, so the 15.5 kg box weighs 15.5 × 1000 = 15 500 g. 500 g of that is the weight of the box, so the books weigh 15 500 – 500 = 15 000 g. If there are 50 books, each book must weigh 15 000 ÷ 50 = 300 g.

Pages 37-38

1) 2:25 or 14:25
The hour hand is between the 2 and the 3, so the hour is 2 o'clock. The minutes hand is pointing to 25 minutes past the hour, so the time is 25 past two.

2) 10 minutes
Clock B shows the time as 2:45, clock C shows the time as 2:55. There are 10 minutes between 2:45 and 2:55.

3) 3:55 or 15:55
Clock D shows the time as ten past three. 45 minutes after this will be 10 + 45 = 55 minutes past three.

4) B
The number of hours will be less than 12 for a time in the morning. The only time where the number of hours is less than 12 is 05:25, so the answer is B.

5) A
The clock showing the latest time will be the clock showing the greatest number of hours. Clock A shows the greatest number of hours (20) and so shows the latest time.

6) C
To change a pm time from the 12-hour clock into the 24-hour clock you need to add 12 to the number of hours. 5 + 12 = 17, so 5:25 pm is 17:25 in the 24-hour clock. This is shown by clock C.

7) D
Twenty five past three is 3:25 in the 12-hour clock or 15:25 in the 24-hour clock. 15:25 is shown by clock D.

8) 3 hours 10 minutes
To find the difference in time you need to count on from 12:15 to 15:25. From 12.15 to 15.15 there are 3 hours. Then 15.15 to 15:25 there are a further 10 minutes. So the difference in time is 3 hours and 10 minutes.

9) D
The number of hours is greater than 12 so 22:17 is in the afternoon (pm). 22 − 12 = 10, so 22:17 in 12-hour clock is 10:17 pm.

10) 10:20
Train C is the latest train that arrives in Northover before 12:00. Train C leaves Southwold at 10:20.

11) 122
March and May both have 31 days. April and June both have 30 days. So in March, April, May and June there are 31 + 30 + 31 + 30 = 122 days.

12) 40 minutes
The easiest way to find the difference in minutes is to count on from the time that Jane was born (8:15) to the time that Susan was born (8:55).
8:15 + 30 minutes takes you to 8:45.
8:45 + 10 minutes takes you to 8:55.
30 + 10 = 40, so Jane is 40 minutes older than Susan.

13) 45 minutes
To find the waiting time you need to count on from 9:25 to 10:10.
9:25 + 5 minutes takes you to 9:30.
9:30 + 30 minutes takes you to 10:00.
10:00 + 10 minutes takes you to 10:10.
5 + 30 + 10 = 45, so you'd have to wait 45 minutes for the Cartoons to start.

14) Wednesday
26 − 9 = 17 so there are 17 days between the 9th and the 26th of January. There are 7 days in a week. 2 × 7 = 14, so 17 days = 2 weeks and 17 − 14 = 3 days. If the 9th is a Sunday, it'll be a Sunday again 2 weeks after that. A further 3 days after that it'll be a Wednesday.

15) 6:10 am
To find the arrival time of the train you need to add one and three quarter hours (1:45) onto 4:25. Start by adding the number of hours. 4:25 + 1 hour = 5:25.
Then add the number of minutes.
Split the 45 minutes into 35 minutes and 10 minutes.
5:25 + 35 minutes = 6:00.
6:00 + 10 minutes = 6:10.
So the train arrives at 6:10 am.

16) April
If Anita eats an apple every day it will take her 100 days to eat 100 apples. January has 31 days and February has 28 days. 28 + 31 = 59. March has 31 days and 59 + 31 = 90, so 10 days into April she'll have had 100 apples. (If it was a leap year, there would be 29 days in February, but it would still be April when Anita had eaten 100 apples.)

17) 13:35
To find the time 35 minutes ago you need to subtract 35 minutes from 14:10. Split the 35 minutes into 10 minutes and 25 minutes.
14:10 − 10 minutes = 14:00. 14:00 − 25 minutes = 13:35.
So the answer is 13:35.

18) 22
There are 31 days in May so there are 31 − 21 = 10 days until the beginning of June. It is then a further 12 days until Sarah's birthday on the 12th. So it is 10 + 12 = 22 days until Sarah's birthday.

19) 9 hours 15 minutes
To find the total time Johnny slept for you need to add the time he slept for on day 1 to the time he slept for on day 2. The time he slept for on day 1 is equal to 12:00 (midnight) − 10:15 = 1:45. The time he slept for on day 2 = 7:30. 1:45 + 7:30 = 9:15, so he slept for 9 hours and 15 minutes.

20) 9:30
To find the time the film finishes you need to add 1 hour 35 minutes onto 7:55 (five to eight).
First add the number of hours. 7:55 + 1 hour = 8:55.
Then add the number of minutes.
Split 35 minutes into 5 minutes and 30 minutes.
8:55 + 5 minutes = 9:00.
9:00 + 30 minutes = 9:30.
So the film finishes at 9:30.

21) 16 hours 30 minutes
From the table, if the letter is posted at 2:30 pm on Thursday, the next collection will be at 7 am on Friday. So the letter will be waiting for 12:00 − 2:30 = 9 hours 30 minutes on Thursday and a further 7 hours on Friday.
That's 9 + 7 = 16 hours and 30 minutes in total.

22) 17 minutes 8 seconds
To find the difference in time you need to count on from Don's time to Ivor's time. Don ran the marathon in 2:29:53.
2:29:53 + 7 seconds = 2:30:00.
2:30:00 + 17 minutes = 2:47:00.
2:47:00 + 1 second = 2:47:01.
7 + 1 = 8, so Don ran the marathon 17 minutes and 8 seconds faster than Ivor.

Answers

Section Seven — Mixed Problems
Pages 39-40

1) £7
Annie is paid £210 in total so divide this by 5 to find the amount of money she earns each day: £210 ÷ 5 = £42. Each day she works from 9 am to 3 pm so she works for 6 hours in total. £42 ÷ 6 = £7, so she earns £7 each hour.

2) 170
Add together Suzy's marks to find her total mark: 48 + 67 + 50 = 165. Then round 165 to the nearest 10 to find her final mark. 165 is exactly half way between 160 and 170. So, according to rounding rules, you round it up and the answer is 170.

3) E
There are three times as many builders in the group of 6 compared to the group of 2, so they will build the houses three times as quickly. It will take the group of 6 builders 24 ÷ 3 = 8 days to build one house, so it will take them 8 × 2 = 16 days to build two houses.

4) 800 s
The container holds 8 litres of water, so to half-fill it you need to add 8 litres ÷ 2 = 4 litres of water. There are 1000 ml in 1 litre, so 4 litres of water is 4 × 1000 = 4000 ml. Divide the total number of millilitres by the amount of water being added each second to find the number of seconds: 4000 ÷ 5 = 800 seconds.

5) E
The diagram below shows the shape. The shape has 6 sides, so it is a hexagon.

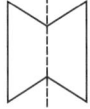

6) 50 minutes
Work out the amount of time Phil spent doing his homework each day.
Monday: 4:15 to 5:15 = 60 minutes.
Tuesday: 5:05 to 5:55 = 50 minutes.
Wednesday: 5:30 to 6:10 = 40 minutes.
To find the average, add the times together and divide by the number of days (3). 60 + 50 + 40 = 150 minutes. 150 ÷ 3 = 50 minutes.

7) 2 hours and 12 minutes
The difference between 14 °C and 25 °C is 25 − 14 = 11 °C. The temperature rises by 1 °C every 12 minutes, so it will take 12 × 11 = 132 minutes to reach 25 °C. There are 60 minutes in 1 hour so there are 2 × 60 = 120 minutes in 2 hours. 132 − 120 = 12, so 132 minutes is 2 hours and 12 minutes.

8) A
There are 24 hours in 1 day, so there are 24 × 2 = 48 hours in 2 days. So, 60 hours is 2 days + 12 hours. Count on from 10:00 am on Friday: 2 days takes you to 10:00 am on Sunday (morning). 12 hours takes you to 10:00 pm on Sunday (evening).

9) D
4 people each collect 2 litres a day, so they collect 4 × 2 litres = 8 litres each day in total. They are camping for 5 days, so they collect 8 litres × 5 = 40 litres in total. The total cost of the water is 40 × 60p = 2400p. 2400p = £24.00.

10) C
Sides a and b in the isosceles triangle are the same length. So to find the perimeter you can double the length of side a and then add the length of side c. This is written as $2a + c$.

11) 48 cm
There are 5 brownies in a row along the board. The length of the 5 brownies is 5 × 8 cm = 40 cm. There is also a 4 cm border around the board, so this adds on 4 cm at each end. So the length of the board is 40 cm + 4 cm + 4 cm = 48 cm.

12) £124
20% of the £155 paid by each person is used to buy food. 10% is £155 ÷ 10 = £15.50, so 20% is £15.50 × 2 = £31. £31 of the £155 is used to buy food, so the amount of money that is not used to buy food is £155 − £31 = £124.

13) 5%
The area of the wall can be found by multiplying the length and height: 4 m × 2.5 m = 10 m². 10% of 10 m² is 10 m² ÷ 10 = 1 m² so 0.5 m² is 10% ÷ 2 = 5%.

14) 6
Add the numbers that she rolled together in throws 1-5 to find her score for each throw:
Throw 1: 2 + 3 = 5
Throw 2: 6 + 1 = 7
Throw 3: 5 + 1 = 6
Throw 4: 4 + 5 = 9
Throw 5: 3 + 6 = 9
Then add the 5 scores together to find the total score for the 5 throws: 5 + 7 + 6 + 9 + 9 = 36. Her mean score for the 6 throws was 7, so her total score for the 6 throws is 7 × 6 = 42. So, her score on the 6th throw was 42 − 36 = 6.

15) $1/8$
Read off the chart to find the number of children who have a birthday in each month, apart from March. Then add the numbers together to find the total number of children who have a birthday in these months: 2 + 3 + 2 + 5 + 3 + 1 + 1 + 4 + 2 + 3 + 2 = 28. There are 32 children in the class, so the remaining children have a birthday in March: 32 − 28 = 4 children. The fraction of children who have a birthday in March is $4/32$. This can be simplified to $1/8$ by dividing the numerator and the denominator by 4.

Assessment Test 1
Pages 41-45

1) 130
To multiply by 1000, move each digit of the number three places to the left: 0.13 → 1.3 → 13 → 130.

2) E
Sixteen thousand and twenty six has a 1 in the ten thousands column, a 6 in the thousands column, 0 in the hundreds column, 2 in the tens column and 6 in the units column. So the number is 16 026. This is option E.

3) D
Compare the place value of the digits in the options. Start with the value of the digits on the left. If these have the same place value and are the same number, compare the values of the next lot of digits to the right until you find the smallest number and place value. 32 is the biggest number because it has a 3 in the tens column. The other four numbers have 3 units, but 3.08 is the only number to have 0 in the tenths column, so the smallest number is 3.08.

4) 2
Rectangles have 1 vertical line of symmetry and 1 horizontal line of symmetry.

5) D
From the options given, the units that can be used to measure length are m, cm and km. m and km are far too big to measure the length of a pencil, so the most sensible unit to use would be cm. This is option D.

6) B
The area of a rectangle is the length × the width. So the area of the tile is 30 cm × 15 cm. Split the 15 cm into 10 cm and 5 cm. 10 × 30 = 300, 5 × 30 = 150, so 30 × 15 = 300 + 150 = 450 cm². This is answer B.

7) 62
The table shows that there are 43 children with long brown hair and 19 children with long black hair. 19 = 20 + 1, so to easily add 19 to 43, you can add 20 then minus 1.
43 + 20 = 63, 63 − 1 = 62. So 62 children had long hair that was either brown or black.

8) (9, 6)

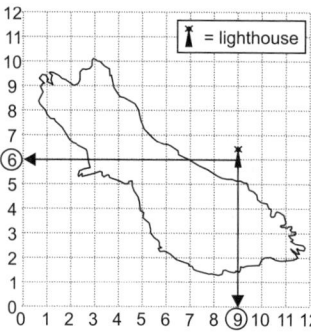

The x-coordinate of the lighthouse is 9. The y-coordinate of the lighthouse is 6. So the coordinate location of the lighthouse is (9, 6).

9) 135
The number of beads she has left is 201 − 66. Split the 66 up into 60, 5 and 1. 201 − 1 = 200. 200 − 60 = 140. 140 − 5 = 135. So, Jamila has 135 beads left.

10) 24 cm
The perimeter is the distance around the outside edge of the shape. Since the triangles are isosceles, each of the outside edges are 3 cm long. There are 8 outside edges so the perimeter is 8 × 3 = 24 cm.

11) B
On the scales, there are 10 divisions between 0 and 0.5, so each division is worth 0.5 ÷ 10 = 0.05 kg. The arrow on the scales is pointing to 3 divisions after 1.5 kg. 3 × 0.05 = 0.15 kg. So the grapes weigh 1.5 + 0.15 = 1.65 kg.

12) 140
On the pie chart, the number of children cycling to school is represented by ¼ of the pie. The number of children walking to school (walking by themselves, or with friends or with parents), is represented by ½ the pie. A half is twice as big as a quarter, so the number of children who walk is 70 × 2 = 140.

13) D
Find the total weight of the basket by adding the weight of the beans and the apples to the weight of the basket. The weight of the apples is 2 × 160. Split the 160 into 100 and 60. 2 × 100 = 200. 2 × 60 = 120. So 2 × 160 = 200 + 120 = 320 g. There are 1000 g in a kg, so the beans weigh 1000 × 1.4 = 1400 g. So the total weight of the basket is 250 + 320 + 1400 = 1970 g or 1.97 kg. This is answer D.

14) 360°
If the floor robot finishes facing the same direction it started in then it must have done 1 full turn. There are 360° degrees in a circle. So it must have turned a full 360°.

15) 67
Split the £3.35 into £3 and 35p. 35 ÷ 5 = 7, so there are seven 5p coins in 35p. There are twenty 5p coins in £1, so in £3 there are 20 × 3 = 60 5p coins. 60 + 7 = 67, so 67 5p coins would be needed to make £3.35.

16) £39
Heike needs 300 tiles. The tiles come in packs of 50, so Heike will need 300 ÷ 50 = 6 packs of tiles. This will cost 6 × £6.50. Split the £6.50 into £6 and 50p. 6 × £6 = £36. 6 × 50p = 300p = £3. So the minimum amount Heike could spend is £36 + £3 = £39.

17) 6
11, 13, 17, 19, 23 and 29 are all prime numbers because their only factors are themselves and one. So there are 6 prime numbers between 10 and 30.

18) 62
Each whole symbol equals 3 bikes, so ⅓ of a symbol equals 1 bike, and ⅔ of a symbol equals 2 bikes.
There are 19 whole symbols = 19 × 3 bikes = 57 bikes, plus 2 times ⅔ of a symbol = 2 × 2 bikes = 4 bikes, plus a ⅓ of a symbol = 1 bike.
Adding them together, you get — 57 + 4 + 1 = 62 bikes.

19) −8 °C
The lowest night time temperature is 26 °C colder than the highest daytime temperature, so the lowest night time temperature is 18 − 26 °C. The difference between 18 °C and 0 °C is 18 °C. 26 − 18 = 8. So the temperature must be a further 8 °C below 0 °C. 0 − 8 = −8 °C. So the lowest night temperature is −8 °C.

20) A
21 ÷ 7 = 3, 210 ÷ 7 = 30, 49 ÷ 7 = 7 and 77 ÷ 7 = 11. The only number that's not a multiple of 7 is 550.

21) 24
There are 360° in the whole cake. From the diagram, each slice is 15° of the cake, so the number of slices will be 360 ÷ 15. Split the 360 into 300 and 60.
300 ÷ 15 = 20. 60 ÷ 15 = 4, so from the whole cake you'd get 20 + 4 = 24 slices.

22) 2 hours 15 minutes
The clock shows that the disco started at 9:30 pm. It finished at 23:45. 23 − 12 = 11, so 23:45 = 11:45 pm. Count on from 9:30 pm to 11:45 pm to find how long the disco lasted. 9:30 pm + 2 hours = 11:30 pm. 11:30 pm + 15 minutes = 11:45 pm. So the disco lasted 2 hours and 15 minutes.

23) 15 g
10% of 25 g = 25 ÷ 10 = 2.5 g. So 20% of 25 g = 2.5 × 2 = 5 g — each biscuit contains 5 g of fat. That means Charlie ate 5 × 3 = 15 g of fat in total.

Answers

24) (–5, 3)

The y-coordinate of point C doesn't change — it's still 3. The x-coordinate changes from 11 to –5. So the coordinate of point C on the reflected triangle is (–5, 3).

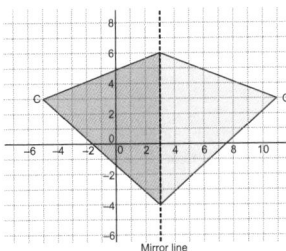

25) E

6.9 × 3.1 is approximately the same as 7 × 3 = 21. So the answer is E.

26) 7 : 9

There are 7 shaded sections and 9 non-shaded sections.

27) 55 ml

On the graph, there are 4 divisions between 0 ml and 20 ml, so each division is worth 20 ÷ 4 = 5 ml. If you draw a line straight up from 6 hours until you reach the line and then straight across, the amount of water is 1 division before 60 ml. So the amount of water in the bucket after 6 hours is 60 – 5 = 55 ml.

28) 41

The side lengths of each layer increase by 1 cube as you move down the tower. So in the next layer there will be 4 × 4 = 16 blocks. In the layer after that there will be 5 × 5 = 25 blocks. So to build the tower two levels higher Josie will need 16 + 25 = 41 blocks.

29) 60 m

There are two classes each with 25 children, so there are 25 × 2 = 50 children in total. 50 is exactly half of 100, so you can work out the amount of wool needed by doing (120 × 100) ÷ 2:
120 × 100 = 12 000, 12 000 ÷ 2 = 6000
There are 100 cm in a metre, so the amount of wool needed is 6000 ÷ 100 = 60 m

30) 13

1 in every 8 mints are spearmint, so in 104 mints there will be 104 ÷ 8 = 13 spearmint mints.

31) 5

The tallest bar is the one showing plants with 5 leaves. So the most common number of leaves must be 5.

32) C

To find $\frac{3}{8}$ of 32 you need to divide 32 by 8 and then multiply it by 3. 32 ÷ 8 = 4, 4 × 3 = 12. So $\frac{3}{8}$ of 32 is 12. This is answer C.

33) 113

For the 56th term, n = 56. 2 × 56 = 112 (2 × 50 = 100, 2 × 6 = 12, 100 + 12 = 112). 112 + 1 = 113, so the 56th term in the sequence is 113.

34) 7

Start by finding the total number of red cars that passed the school. Read off the values for each hour from the graph and add them together: 12 + 9 + 6 + 5 + 8 + 7 + 4 + 5 = 56. There were 8 hours in total, so the mean number of red cars in an hour is 56 ÷ 8 = 7.

35) A

For the three hours that Richard spent gardening he earned £5.20 × 3. £5.20 is only 20p more than £5.00, so £5.20 × 3 = £5.00 × 3 + 20p × 3 = £5.00 × 3 + 60p. For the 4½ hours Richard spent cleaning he earned 4.5 × £4.80. Split the 4.5 into 4 and 0.5. 4.5 × £4.80 = 4 × £4.80 + 0.5 × £4.80 = 4 × £4.80 + £2.40. So the total amount Richard was paid was £5.00 × 3 + 60p + 4 × £4.80 + £2.40. This is answer A.

36) 16 cm²

A cube has 12 edges, so the length of each edge is 48 ÷ 12 = 4 cm. The faces of a cube are a square, so the area of each face is 4 × 4 = 16 cm².

37) D

The area of the yard is 0.2 × 7.
2 × 7 = 14, 0.2 is 10 times smaller than 2, so 0.2 × 7 = 14 ÷ 10 = 1.4 m².
Volume = depth × area = $\frac{1}{10}$ × 1.4 = 1.4 ÷ 10 = 0.14 m³

38) B

64 = 32 × 2, so 32 × 1322 = (64 × 1322) ÷ 2.
64 × 1322 = 84 608,
so 32 × 1322 = 84 608 ÷ 2 = 42 304. This is answer B.

39) C

The £2 fee is only charged once. The 30p charge is multiplied by the number of kms (Y). There are 100 pence in £1, so 30p = 30 ÷ 100 = £0.3. So the cost of the fare is £2 + £0.3Y. This is answer C.

40) 5

One adult is needed per six children, so the total number of adults needed is 162 ÷ 6. Using short division, 162 ÷ 6 = 27, so there will be 27 adults as well as the 162 children. In total there will be 162 + 27 people. Split the 27 into 20 and 7. 162 + 20 = 182. 182 + 7 = 189. So there will be 189 people on the trip.
Counting up in 42s, one coach holds 42 people, two coaches will hold 84 people. three coaches will hold 126 people, four coaches will hold 168 people and five coaches will hold 210 people. You can't have half a coach and four coaches won't be enough, so five coaches will be needed in total.

Assessment Test 2
Pages 46-51

1) 53 024

There should be a 5 in the ten thousands column, a 3 in the thousands column, there are no hundreds so there should be a zero in the hundreds column, a 2 in the tens column and a 4 in the units.

2) D

45 + 30 + 25 = 100, so the answer is D.

3) A

Each of these shapes have 5 sides, so they're pentagons.

4) D

An adult usually weighs between 50 kg and 100 kg. A horse usually weighs a lot more, so options A, B, C and E are too light. So option D (400 kg) is the best estimate.

5) £1.79

The cheapest way for Mark to send the items is second class. A parcel weighing 100 – 250 g costs 110p, so this will be the cost of sending the 180 g parcel. The 90 g parcel is less than 100 g, and so will cost 69p to send second class. The total minimum cost = 69 + 110 = 179p = £1.79

6) 160
The sequence so far has been add 1, add 2, add 3, add 4. So to get the next number in the sequence you need to add 5. Adding 5 onto 155 gives 160, so this is the next number in the sequence.

7) B
To go in the shaded area of the Venn diagram the number must be a factor of 24 and a factor of 105. $24 \div 3 = 8$ and $105 \div 3 = 35$, so the answer is B.

8) D
There are 20 tiles in total. 5 of these are shaded, so $5/20$ of the tiles are shaded. To convert a fraction into a percentage you need to create an equivalent fraction which has denominator of 100. $5/20$ is the same as $25/100$ if you multiply the numerator and the denominator by 5. $25/100$ is 25%. Alternatively, there are 4 rows of tiles. The equivalent of one whole row is shaded. This is $1/4$ of the tiles. $1/4 = 25\%$.

9) 9600
400 is 100 times bigger than 4. So 24×400 is the same as $(24 \times 4) \times 100$. You're told that $24 \times 4 = 96$, so $24 \times 400 = 96 \times 100 = 9600$.

10) E
Bicycle wheels usually have a circumference that's more than a metre, but much less than 17 m, so the only realistic measurement from the options is 1.7 m. This is answer E.

11) 1 and 5
Shape 5 is shape 1 rotated 90° clockwise.

12) D
23:35 is 25 minutes to midnight. The next closest time to midnight is 00:35, which is 35 minutes past midnight — 10 minutes further away from midnight than 23:35. So the answer is D.

13) Buttercups
On the graph, there are bars that show 15, 36, 30 and 17 flowers, but there is no bar showing 19 flowers. There were 19 buttercups, so buttercups haven't been drawn on the graph yet.

14) D
From the pie chart, less than $1/4$ of children wear full school uniform. The only option that is less than $1/4$ is $1/6$, so the answer is D.

15) 21 °C
Count up from −16 °C to 5 °C to find the difference in temperature. Add 16 to get from −16 °C to 0 °C. Add 5 to get from 0 °C to 5 °C. $16 + 5 = 21$, so Quebec was 21 °C colder than England.

16) 14 cm²
The grid is 7 cm by 4 cm, so it has an area of $7 \text{ cm} \times 4 \text{ cm} = 28 \text{ cm}^2$. The triangle takes up half of the grid, so it has an area of $28 \text{ cm}^2 \div 2 = 14 \text{ cm}^2$.

17) E
177 is the only number from those given that divides by 3 without leaving a remainder. So it is a multiple of 3.
A quick way of checking whether a number is a multiple of 3 is to add the digits together. The number is only a multiple of 3 if the digits add up to a multiple of 3. The digits in 177 add up to 15 $(1 + 7 + 7 = 15)$. 15 is a multiple of 3 $(5 \times 3 = 15)$, so 177 is a multiple of 3 too.

18) 6
From the table, there are 21 pages that have 6 pictures. That's more pages than for any other number of pictures, so the most common number of pictures on a page is 6.

19) D
$17/2$ is the same as $17 \div 2$. $17 = 16 + 1$. $16 \div 2 = 8$. $1 \div 2 = 0.5$. $8 + 0.5 = 8.5$.

20) B
A right-angle is 90°. Looking at the diagram, angle B is the closest to 90°. The corners of a piece of paper are all 90°, so you can use the corner of a piece of paper to check how close to a right-angle an angle is.

21) 6 hours
Each symbol on the pictogram shows 4 hours of rain. So each $1/4$ of a symbol = 1 hour of rain. There are $5 1/4$ symbols for Monday, so on Monday there were 5×4 hours + 1 hour = 21 hours of rain. There are $3 3/4$ symbols for Thursday, so on Thursday there were 3×4 hours + 3 hours = 15 hours of rain. $21 - 15 = 6$, so there were 6 more hours of rain on Monday than on Thursday. Alternatively, find how many more symbols there are for Monday than there are for Thursday: $5 1/4 - 3 3/4 = 1 1/2$. Then work out the number of hours of rain represented by these symbols: 1×4 hours + 2 hours = 6.

22) 1500 g
Making 25 flapjacks that each need 20 g of sugar will use $25 \times 20 = 500$ g of sugar in total. There are 1000 g in a kilogram, so a 2 kg bag of sugar will contain $2 \times 1000 = 2000$ g of sugar. Using 500 g will leave $2000 - 500 = 1500$ g of sugar in the bag.

23) 8 years
M = 1000, C = 100, X = 10 and I = 1.
A smaller numeral before a larger one represents the difference between the two, so: CM = 1000 − 100 = 900, XC = 100 − 10 = 90 and IX = 10 − 1 = 9. So the numerals represent: $1000 + 900 + 90 + 9 = 1999$. Niamh was born in 2007, so the film is $2007 - 1999 = 8$ years older than Niamh.

24) B
A parallelogram has two pairs of equal parallel sides. So the fourth corner must be at (2, 2).

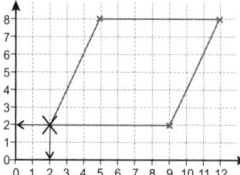

25) £3
The difference between waffle cones and normal cones is $46p - 36p = 10p$. Sanji wants to buy 30 ice cream cones, so that's $10p \times 30 = 300p$, or £3. So it costs £3 more to buy waffle cones instead of normal cones.
Alternatively you could work out total cost of buying 30 normal cones and 30 waffle cones. Buying 30 waffle cones will cost $30 \times 46p$. Split the 46p into 40p and 6p. $30 \times 40 = 1200$. $30 \times 6 = 180$. So $30 \times 46 = 1200 + 180 = 1380p$. Buying 30 normal cones will cost $30 \times 36p$. Split the 36p into 30p and 6p. $30 \times 30 = 900p$. $30 \times 6 = 180p$. So $30 \times 36 = 900 + 180 = 1080p$. $1380 - 1080 = 300p$ or £3.

26) D
When the net is folded into a cube it will look like this:
The arrow is pointing to side D.

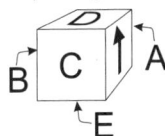

27) 872.6
872.63 has 6 tenths. To round this to the nearest tenth, look at the next digit to the right of the tenths position — this is 3.
3 is less than 5, so round down to 872.6.

28) 42
You need to work out 378 ÷ 9.
$$9 \overline{)3^37^18}$$
with quotient 4 2

29) 38 cm
Eight 2 cm widths, two 8 cm lengths and six 1 cm bits make up the perimeter:
So the perimeter is
(8 × 2 cm) + (2 × 8 cm) + (6 × 1 cm)
= 16 cm + 16 cm + 6 cm = 38 cm.

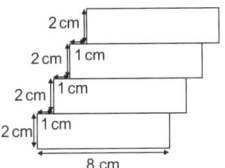

30) £1.30
1 large pack and 2 smalls packs will cost
£15 + £5.50 + £5.50 = £26 in total. The mean price per mug
= the total cost ÷ the number of mugs purchased.
Caleb bought 1 large pack and 2 small packs, so that is
12 + 4 + 4 = 20 mugs in total. The mean cost of 1 mug is
£26 ÷ 20. £26 ÷ 2 = £13, so £26 ÷ 20 = £1.30.
So the mean price per mug is £1.30.

31) 25 °C
On the graph, the highest temperature reached is 16 °C.
The lowest temperature reached is −9 °C.
−9 °C is 9 °C below 0, and 16 °C is 16 degrees above 0.
So the difference between them is 9 + 16 = 25 °C.

32) £2.11
Buying 6 postcards at 49p each will cost 6 × 49p. Round 49p to 50p to make the calculation easier: 6 × 50p = £3.
You've rounded up the cost of 6 postcards by 1p each, so £3 is 6 × 1p = 6p too much. Buying 5 postcards at 99p each will cost 5 × 99p. This is approximately 5 × £1 = £5. This is 5 × 1p = 5p too much. So the total cost is £3 + £5 − 6p − 5p = £8 − 11p = £7.89. Count up to £10 to work out Sandy's change:
£7.89 + 11p = £8, £8 + £2 = £10.
So her change = 11p + £2 = £2.11.

33) B
From the diagram, Nico put 150 ml of squash into the measuring jug. So 150 ml = 1 measure. Nico needs to add 5 measures of water, which is 150 × 5 = 750 ml of water. This will give 150 + 750 = 900 ml of diluted squash in total. There are 1000 ml in a litre so 900 ml = 900 ÷ 1000 = 0.9 l.

34) 340 miles
A car travels 8.5 miles on one litre of fuel. So on 40 litres of fuel, it will travel 40 × 8.5 miles. Split the 8.5 into 8 and 0.5. 40 × 8 = 320. 0.5 × 8 = 20. 320 + 20 = 340.
So the car can travel 340 miles.

35) C
There are 10 divisions between 3.5 and 4.0.
So 10 divisions = 4.0 − 3.5 = 0.5.
This means each division = 0.5 ÷ 10 = 0.05. Counting along the number line divisions in steps of 0.05 shows that Y lies between 3.70 and 3.75, so statement C is correct.

36) 40°
There are 180° along a straight line.
So angle k = 180° − 76° − 64° = 40°.

37) £10.40
If each phone call lasts two minutes, each call to a landline will cost 12p × 2 = 24p and each call to a mobile will cost 25p × 2 = 50p. Joe rings 10 friends on landlines, which costs 24 × 10 = 240p. He rings 16 friends on mobile phones, which costs 50p × 16 = 800p. So in total, Joe's calls will cost 240 + 800 = 1040p = £10.40.

38) A
Both of the fractions $^8/_{12}$ and $^6/_9$ simplify to $^2/_3$. You divide the number on the top and the number on the bottom of $^8/_{12}$ by 4, and the number on the top and the number on the bottom of $^6/_9$ by 3. So $^8/_{12}$ and $^6/_9$ are equivalent.

39) 54 cm
The side lengths of the hexagons increase by 1 cm each time. The 3rd hexagon in the sequence has side lengths of 6 cm, so the 6th hexagon will have side lengths of 6 cm + 3 cm = 9 cm. Regular hexagons have 6 sides of the same length, so the perimeter of the 6th hexagon will be 6 × 9 cm = 54 cm.

40) E
If Lewis rode Y miles, Tom rode twice as far = 2Y miles.
So, the total distance ridden by the two boys is
Y miles + 2Y miles = 3Y miles.

Assessment Test 3
Pages 52-56

1) 0.59
To make the smallest number possible you need to arrange the digits in order from smallest to biggest. So the smallest number is 0.59.

2) 28
Each block of lines on the tally chart is 5 points. For Team 4, the chart shows 5 blocks of lines plus three individual lines. This is a total of 5 × 5 + 3 = 28.

3) D
The last two digits in the telephone number add up to 10, so the second missing digit must be 8 (2 + 8 = 10).
Add up the 10 digits now known and subtract this from 40 to find the first missing digit:
0 + 7 + 0 + 7 + 0 + 3 + 6 + 4 + 2 + 8 = 37.
40 − 37 = 3, so the two missing digits are 3 and 8.

4) 13 mm
A regular pentagon has 5 sides that are an equal length, so divide the perimeter (65 mm) by 5 to find the length of one side:
$$5 \overline{)6^15}$$
with quotient 1 3. The answer is 13 mm.

5) L
Reflex angles are larger than two right angles (the angle along a straight line). So angle L is a reflex angle.

6) D

In one minute there are 60 seconds and in 1 hour there are 60 minutes, so the number of seconds in 1 hour is 60 × 60. Use the times table fact 6 × 6 = 36 to work this out: 60 is ten times bigger than 6 so the answer to 60 × 60 will be 10 × 10 = 100 times bigger than 36. 36 × 100 = 3600. So there are 3600 seconds in 1 hour.

7) 41

Find the information you need in the table. There are 15 comedy films with a U rating and 11 with a PG rating, so Steph can see 15 + 11 = 26 comedy films in total. There are 7 action films with a U rating and 8 with a PG rating so she can see 7 + 8 = 15 action films in total. So altogether Steph can see 26 + 15 = 41 films.

8) £24

10% of £10 is £10 ÷ 10 = £1, so 20% of £10 is 2 × £1 = £2. This means the cost of a CD is £10 − £2 = £8. So 3 CDs will cost 3 × £8 = £24.

9) D

Work out each option until you find the one that gives 690. 694 rounds to 690 to the nearest 10 (option D). 694 is between 690 and 700, and the 4 is less than 5, so it rounds down to 690.

10) 60

4^3 = 4 × 4 × 4 = 16 × 4 = 64.
So Elsie's grandmother is 64 − 4 = 60 years older than Elsie.

11) B

Count up 28°C from −4°C to find the temperature inside.

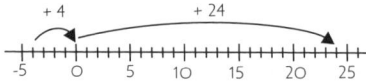

Add 4°C to get from −4°C to 0. There is 24°C left to add (28 − 4 = 24). This brings the temperature to 24°C. Thermometer B shows 24 °C.

12) C

6 eggs cost £1, milk costs 99p and cheese costs £2.29. So you need to add £1 + 99p + 99p + £2.29. Round up the price of the milk to £1 and the cheese to £2.30 to give an easier calculation: £1 + £1 + £1 + £2.30 = £5.30. You rounded up 3 items up by 1p each so subtract 3p to get the final answer: £5.30 − 3p = £5.27.

13) 10

In each shape there are 2 more black tiles than in the shape before. In the 5th shape there are 8 black tiles, so in the 6th shape there will be 8 + 2 = 10 black tiles.

14) D

Out of the numbers given, only 24 and 30 are multiples of 3 (these are in the three times table whereas 4, 10 and 16 are not). 30 × 3 = 90, so 30 is a factor of 90. (24 × 4 = 96, so 24 is not a factor of 90).

15) A

The semi-circle is made up of two identical quarter-circles, so estimate the area of one of these quarter-circles and then multiply by 2. There are 13 whole squares and 4 half squares (ignore the two squares which are only a tiny bit inside the circle), so the quarter-circle has an area of around
13 + (4 × ½) = 13 + 2 = 15 cm².

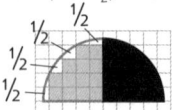

So the area of the semi-circle must be around
15 cm² × 2 = 30 cm². This is answer option A.

16) 62

310 is one-third of 930 (930 ÷ 3 = 310). So 310 ÷ 5 will be one-third of 930 ÷ 5. 930 ÷ 5 = 186, so divide 186 by 3 to find the answer. 186 splits into 180 + 6. 180 ÷ 3 = 60, 6 ÷ 3 = 2. So 310 ÷ 5 = 60 + 2 = 62.

17) 4 : 1

There were 4 red cars and 1 silver car. So the ratio of red cars to silver cars is 4 : 1.

18) E

> means 'is bigger than' so Z must be a number that's bigger than 211.55. The only option that is bigger than 211.55 is 211.7 — option E.

19) C

100 ÷ 25 = 4, so 700 ÷ 25 will give an answer 7 times larger: 7 × 4 = 28. 709 is 700 + 9, so 709 ÷ 25 = 28 remainder 9.

20) D

Visualise the nets being folded and check that there are faces in the correct positions. When net D is folded, one of the small square faces overlaps with one of the rectangular faces, so it doesn't make a closed cuboid.

21) D

Each term of the sequence is 0.5 less than the previous term. So the next number in the sequence is 0.75 − 0.5 = 0.25.

22) B

A 30 cm candle is equivalent to fifteen 2 cm sections (15 × 2 = 30). So a 30 cm candle will burn for 15 × 13 minutes. You can work this out by partitioning 13 into 10 + 3 and multiplying each part by 15. 10 × 15 = 150, 3 × 15 = 45, 150 + 45 = 195. So a 30 cm candle will burn for 195 minutes.

23) £8.97

The children's tickets cost 24 × 25p. You can work this out by partitioning 24 into 20 + 4 and multiplying each part by 25: 20 × 25 = 500, 4 × 25 = 100. 500 + 100 = 600 = £6. Each adult ticket costs 99p and there are 3 adults so work out 3 × 99p: Round 99p up to £1 and then multiply by 3: 3 × £1 = £3. The price of each of the three adult tickets was rounded up by 1p, so subtract 3p to find the total cost of the adult tickets: £3 − 3p = £2.97. So the total cost of the bus fares is £6 + £2.97 = £8.97.

24) 8

There are 100 plants that each need 160 ml of water so Jo needs 100 × 160 ml = 16 000 ml of water. There are 1000 ml in 1 litre, so 16 000 ml is 16 litres (16 000 ÷ 1000 = 16). The watering can holds 2 litres of water so Jo will need to fill it 8 times to have enough water (8 × 2 litres = 16 litres).

25) B

You need to imagine how the model would look from behind. Option E shows the model when viewed from the back.

26) E

24 fairy cakes need 200 g of butter, so 12 fairy cakes need 100 g of butter (12 is half of 24, so 12 cakes need half of 200 g of butter). 1 kg = 1000 g, so 2.5 kg = 2.5 × 1000 g = 2500 g. 2500 g is 25 lots of 100 g (25 × 100 = 2500), so there is enough butter to make 25 × 12 = 300 fairy cakes.

27) 120°

The total angle on a circular clock is 360°. The sections between the 12 numbers on the clock are each 360 ÷ 12 = 30°. At twenty-five past twelve the minute hand will be pointing at 5 so will have turned through 4 sections. This is 4 × 30° = 120°.

28) 100 miles
Read the values from the graph. They reached Town C after they had travelled 140 miles and they reached Town D after they had travelled 240 miles. So they travelled a distance of
240 − 140 = 100 miles.

29) C
There are 1000 g in 1 kg, so 1.4 kg is 1.4 × 1000 = 1400 g.
10 bars of chocolate would weigh 10 × 70 g = 700 g.
700 g × 2 = 1400 g so there are 10 × 2 = 20 bars in the box.

30) C
To find the mean, add up the number of words in each question and divide by the number of questions (4).
Total number of words = 27 + 33 + 38 + 26 = 124.
The mean number of words is 124 ÷ 4 = 31.

31) 29
You can see four side faces on each die. These are made up of two pairs of opposite faces, which each add up to 7. So Megan can see 2 × 7 = 14 dots on the side faces of each die. So, on the side faces of the 2 dice she can see 2 × 14 = 28 dots. Megan can see one more dot on top of the top dice, so she can see 28 + 1 = 29 dots in total.

32) 90 units
In 150 hours the fridge uses 150 × 0.6 units. You can work this out by splitting 150 into 100 + 50 and then multiplying each part by 0.6. 100 × 0.6 = 60. 50 × 0.6 is half of 100 × 0.6 (because 50 = 100 ÷ 2), so it is 60 ÷ 2 = 30. So in total the fridge uses 60 + 30 = 90 units over 150 hours.

33) D
1/3 of each shaded paving stone is grey, so split each paving stone into thirds and count the number of sections that are shaded. There are 8 paving stones so 8 × 3 = 24 sections in total. Of these sections, 4 are grey so the fraction of the path that is grey is 4/24. This can be simplified by dividing the numerator and denominator by 4 to give 1/6.

34) 4
Jane uses 20 sweets and alternates the colours so she will need 10 green sweets and 10 orange sweets in total.
In 3 packets of sweets there will be enough orange sweets (3 × 4 = 12) but not enough green sweets (3 × 3 = 9).
So Jane will need to buy 4 packets of sweets.

35) 96 litres
There are 24 hours in 1 day, so the number of times that the water will fill the bowl in 1 day is 24 ÷ 3 = 8. The bowl holds 12 litres of water, so 12 × 8 = 96 litres of water is lost from the pipe in a day.

36) (3, 1)
The diagram shows the triangle after it has been reflected. The coordinates of corner A are now (3, 1).

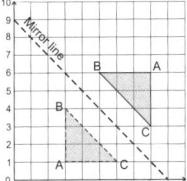

37) 160 litres
A cube with sides of 10 cm has a volume of 10 × 10 × 10 = 1000 cm³. So you can hold 1 litre of water in 1000 cm³. 1 m = 100 cm, so the cuboid has sides of 100 cm, 80 cm and 20 cm. It has a volume of 80 × 20 × 100 = 160 000 cm³. So this cuboid can hold 160 000 ÷ 1000 = 160 litres.

38) E
The shaded sections on the pie chart show the children that are wearing gloves. The shaded sections cover approximately 3/4 of the area of the pie chart. When you write 3/4 as a percentage, it is 75%.

39) B
An octagonal prism has 8 rectangular faces and one octagonal face at each end (2 in total). The area of each rectangular face is R, so the total area of the rectangular faces is 8R. The area of each octagonal face is C, so the total area of the octagonal faces is 2C. So the total area of all the faces is 8R + 2C.

40) 324 m
The 27 m tape measure fits 4 times along the length, and twice along the width. As this diagram shows, the perimeter is made up of 4 + 4 + 2 + 2 = 12 tape measure lengths.

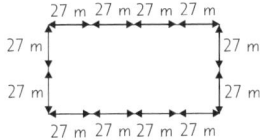

So the perimeter of the field is 12 × 27 m. Work this out by partitioning the 12 into 10 + 2 and multiplying each part by 27 m separately:
10 × 27 m = 270 m
2 × 27 m = 54 m
270 m + 54 m = 324 m.

Assessment Test 4
Pages 57-61

1) D
0.57 and 0.23 are the smallest two numbers, because they have 0 units. 0.57 has five tenths and 0.23 has two tenths, so the smallest number is 0.23.

2) Hamid
The youngest child will have been born most recently. 1999 was after 1997, so the youngest child must be either Archie, Damien or Hamid. Hamid was born in December which is later in the year than January or June, so Hamid is the youngest.

3) 97 412
To make the largest number possible you need to arrange the digits in order from largest to smallest. For the number to be even, you need to have 2 or 4 as the last digit. As 2 is smaller than 4, this is the last digit. So, the largest even number possible is 97 412.

4) D
There are 100 centimetres in 1 metres,
and 10 millimetres in every centimetre, so there are 100 × 10 = 1000 millimetres in 1 metre. So in 3.5 metres there are 3.5 × 1000 = 3500 mm — so the answer is D.

5) E
The shape has six sides, so it's a hexagon.

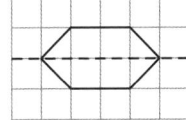

6) C
For 5 to divide exactly into a number the number must end in 5 or 0. Liam's number gives a remainder of 3, so the number must end in 5 + 3 = 8, or 0 + 3 = 3. The only answer that ends in 8 or 3 is 23.

7) £12
25% is the same as $\frac{1}{4}$. $\frac{1}{4}$ of 16 is £16 ÷ 4 = £4. Subtract this from £16 to find the sale price. £16 − £4 = £12.

8) 105
Reading off the graph, 180 books were borrowed from the library on Monday, 60 books were borrowed on Tuesday, 140 books were borrowed on Wednesday, and 40 books were borrowed on Thursday. So the total number of books borrowed was 180 + 60 + 140 + 40 = 420. There were 4 days, so the mean is 420 ÷ 4 = 105.

9) A
There are five fifths in 1 ($\frac{5}{5}$ = 1). In 5 there are 25 fifths (5 × 5).

10) 25p
To find the cost of each apple you need to work out £2.50 ÷ 10 = £0.25 — which is 25p.

11) C
Line N and Line R are at right angles to each other, so they are perpendicular.

12) A
A right angle is 90° and angle y is about half a right angle. 90° ÷ 2 = 45°.

13) 24 °C
Count up from −3 to 21 to find the difference between the two temperatures.

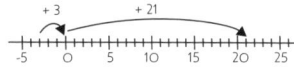

Add 3 to get from −3 to 0. Add 21 to get from 0 to 21. 3 + 21 = 24 °C.

14) 12
Each symbol on the pictogram means 6 doors. There are $4\frac{1}{2}$ symbols for black doors and $2\frac{1}{2}$ symbols for blue doors, so you need to find the difference between them. $4\frac{1}{2} − 2\frac{1}{2}$ = 2 symbols. So there are 2 × 6 = 12 more black doors than blue doors. (Or you could work out the number of doors which are blue and black, and then find the difference. There are $2\frac{1}{2}$ symbols for blue doors. 2 × 6 = 12 and $\frac{1}{2}$ of 6 is 3. So there are 12 + 3 = 15 blue doors. There are $4\frac{1}{2}$ symbols for black doors. 4 × 6 = 24 and $\frac{1}{2}$ of 6 is 3. So there are 24 + 3 = 27 black doors. The difference between the number of blue and black doors is 27 − 15 = 12 doors.)

15) B
The weight of a pencil is approximately 10 g. So 7 g is too light to be the weight of a guinea pig, as is 17.5 g. 75 kg is the weight of an average adult and 700 kg is even heavier, so both of these weights are too heavy for a guinea pig. 750 g is the only realistic answer.

16) 100 m
The playground is rectangular, so it must have two sides of 18 m and two sides of 7 m. 7 + 18 + 7 + 18 = 50 m. Chris ran around the perimeter of the playground twice, which is 2 × 50 m = 100 m.

17) 52
468 is two times bigger than 234. So the answer to 468 ÷ 9 will be 2 times bigger than 26. 26 × 2 = 52.

18) A
To find the number Pat started with you need to work backwards from 64. She squared a number to get 64. This number must have been 8 (8 × 8 = 64). To get 8, Pat multiplied her starting number by 4, so do the opposite and divide 8 by 4 to find the starting number: 8 ÷ 4 = 2.

19) 8 kg
Each right angle is 90° so 270° is 270 ÷ 90 = 3 right angles. When you rotate the pointer clockwise through 3 right angles the weighing scale will show 8 kg.

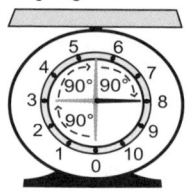

20) D
```
    2 0.7
  ×     6
  1 2 4.2
        4
```
The answer is 124.2.

21) 7
The number of children who like both Chinese and Italian food is shown in the middle section of the Venn diagram (3) and in the section that overlaps the Chinese food circle and the Italian food circle (4). So this is 3 + 4 = 7 children in total.

22) 300 g
To make 10 pies you need 200 g of flour, so to make 5 pies, which is half of 10, you would need 200 g ÷ 2 = 100 g of flour. This means that to make 15 pies you need 200 g + 100 g = 300 g of flour.

23) 50%
Read from the table to find the total number of teams: 3 + 2 + 2 + 2 + 1 = 10 teams in total. The teams who scored more than 2 goals scored either 3, 4 or 5 goals, so 2 + 2 + 1 = 5 teams scored more than 2 goals. 5 teams out of 10 teams scored more than 2 goals, so this is 50% as a percentage.

24) 24
To find the number of pages that are sports pages, find $\frac{2}{5}$ of 40. 40 ÷ 5 = 8, 8 × 2 = 16. There are 16 pages that are sports pages, so there are 40 − 16 = 24 pages that are not.

25) 5 m²
The total area of the car park is 10 × 5 = 50 m². The area needed by each space is 5 × 3 = 15 m², so 3 spaces need 3 × 15 = 45 m². So, the area of the car park left over is 50 − 45 = 5 m².

26) 390 seconds
Jeanne walked for 1 + $5\frac{1}{2}$ = $6\frac{1}{2}$ minutes in total. There are 60 seconds in 1 minute. So you need to work out $6\frac{1}{2}$ × 60. You can split $6\frac{1}{2}$ into 6 + $\frac{1}{2}$ and multiply both by 60. 6 × 60 = 360 seconds. $\frac{1}{2}$ × 60 = 30 seconds. 360 + 30 = 390 seconds.

27) 36
The 5th number in Martha's sequence is 12 − 2 = 10, 10 × 2 = 20. The 6th number will be 20 − 2 = 18, 18 × 2 = 36.

28) A
For A, the mean is (6 + 8 + 8 + 9 + 9) ÷ 5 = 40 ÷ 5 = 8.
For B, the mean is (8 + 4 + 9 + 5 + 4) ÷ 5 = 30 ÷ 5 = 6.
For C, the mean is (2 + 4 + 8 + 5 + 6) ÷ 5 = 25 ÷ 5 = 5.
For D, the mean is (4 + 4 + 8 + 10 + 9) ÷ 5 = 35 ÷ 5 = 7.
For E, the mean is (7 + 5 + 12 + 5 + 6) ÷ 5 = 35 ÷ 5 = 7.
So A has the greatest mean.

29) 1 : 3
Alice has 12 chocolates and 3 of them are coffee creams, so 12 − 3 = 9 must be strawberry creams. This means the ratio of coffee creams to strawberry creams is 3 : 9. Simplify your answer by dividing both sides by 3, giving 1 : 3.

30) C
The point (2, 3) is not inside the shaded circle (see the diagram).

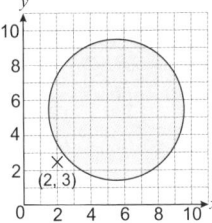

31) E
1.5 litres = 1500 ml. 3 × 1500 ml = 4500 ml, so he has 4500 ml in total. 250 ml × 4 = 1000 ml, or 1 litre. 1 litre of water will fill four 250 ml glasses, so 4 litres will fill 4 × 4 = 16 glasses. There are 500 ml left over which can fill 2 more glasses (2 × 250 ml = 500 ml). So Rodrigo can fill 16 + 2 = 18 glasses.

32) B
You need to find total number of children who swam, so you need to look at the heights of all of the bars. 5 children swam 1 length, 7 children swam 2 lengths, 9 children swam 3 lengths, 5 children swam 4 lengths and 3 children swam 5 lengths.
5 + 7 + 9 + 5 + 3 = 29. There are 30 children in the class so 30 − 29 = 1 child did not swim.

33) £1.20
Manjit received £2.80 in change from £10, so she spent £10 − £2.80 = £7.20 in total. That means that 6 cartons of apple juice cost £7.20, so 1 carton of apple juice costs £7.20 ÷ 6 = £1.20.

34) 36
The shaded section on the pie chart below shows the number of people who went to Turkey. The shaded section covers 1/4 of the area of the pie chart. 12 people went to Turkey, so the total number of people asked is 12 × 4 = 48. This means that the number of people who didn't go to Turkey is 48 − 12 = 36.

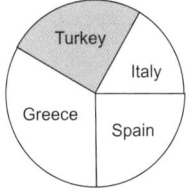

35) B
To find the volume of a cuboid you need to work out the length × width × height. This is 8 × 2 × 2.5. It is easiest to multiply 2 by 2.5 first. 8 × (2 × 2.5) = 8 × 5 = 40.
The volume is 40 cm³.

36) C
Ahmed wants to be in Birmingham for 13:15. The 11:45 bus is the latest bus that Ahmed can take from Henley (it arrives in Birmingham at 13:00). It takes Ahmed 10 minutes to walk from his home to the bus stop. So, the latest time Ahmed should leave home is 10 minutes before 11:45, which is 11:35.

37) E
Count down from 10 in steps of 2¼ until you reach one of the given numbers: 10, 7¾, 5½, 3¼, 1...

38) 65°
There are 180° in a straight line. There are two given angles, one is a right angle, which is 90°, and the other is 25°.
So angle h = 180° − 90° − 25° = 65°.

39) E
The circumference of a wheel is the distance around the edge of the wheel. The wheel makes 7 complete turns so it rolls 7 × 85.5 cm.

```
    8 5.5
×     7
—————
  5 9 8.5
    3 3
```
The wheel rolls 598.5 cm.

40) A
1 dress costs £X and 1 dress costs £Y. So the cost of these two dresses in pounds can be shown as X + Y. 3 blouses each cost £Z, so the cost of these 3 blouses in pounds can be shown as 3Z. The total amount Magdalena spends in pounds can be shown by the expression X + Y + 3Z.

Assessment Test 5
Pages 62-66

1) 15 000
5 × 3 = 15, so 5 × 3000 = 15 000.

2) 3
One shelf can hold 50 DVDs, so 2 shelves will hold 2 × 50 = 100 DVDs. This isn't enough to hold all 136 of Topi's DVDs. 3 shelves will hold 3 × 50 = 150 DVDs. This is enough to hold all 136 of Topi's DVDs, so Topi needs 3 shelves.

3) (6, 5)
The x-coordinate of corner C is 6. The y-coordinate of corner C is 5. So the coordinates of corner C are (6, 5).

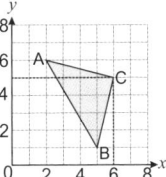

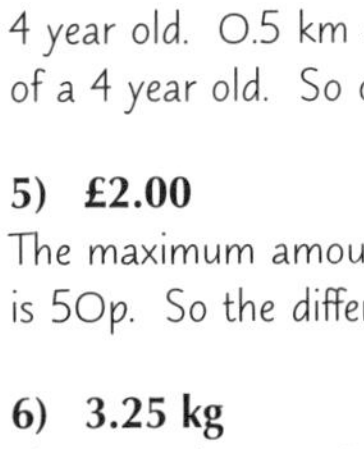

4) E
40 cm and 80 mm are far too small to be the height of a 4 year old. 0.5 km and 2 m are too big to be the height of a 4 year old. So option E is the most likely answer.

5) £2.00
The maximum amount is £2.50 and the minimum amount is 50p. So the difference is £2.50 − 50p = £2.00.

6) 3.25 kg
There are 4 spaces between 0 and 1 kg so each space on the scale is worth 1 kg ÷ 4 = 0.25 kg. The pointer is pointing to a line that is 1 space after 3 kg, so it is pointing to 3kg + 0.25 kg = 3.25 kg.

7) £14.97
To buy 75 pencils you need to buy 3 boxes (3 × 25 = 75). Each box costs £4.99, so the total cost of 75 pencils is 3 × £4.99. £4.99 is only 1p less than £5.00, so
3 × £4.99 = 3 × £5.00 − 3p.
3 × £5.00 = £15.00.
£15.00 − 3 p = £14.97.

8) D
From the options given, km^3, m^3 and ml can be used to measure volumes. ml are far too small to be used to measure the volume of water in a swimming pool. km^3 are far too large, so the best unit to use would be m^3.

9) 2
There are 7 days in a week, so in 3 weeks there are 3 × 7 = 21 days. Mrs Brown feeds her cat two packets of food a day, so in three weeks she will use 21 × 2 = 42 packets of food. In one box of food there are 24 packets — this is not enough to last three weeks. In two boxes of food there are 2 × 24 = 48 packets — this is enough to last three weeks. So Mrs Brown needs to buy 2 boxes of food.

10) C
Each step needs 18 + 20 = 38 cm of carpet. There are 4 steps, so in total 4 × 38 cm of carpet is needed. You can estimate this by rounding 38 cm up to 40 cm. The length needed will be around 4 × 40 = 160 cm. You rounded up so the actual length will be just short of 160 cm (it will be 152 cm). So the answer is C.

11) D
4 squares east from the supermarket takes you to (7, 3), 2 squares south from (7, 3) takes you to the chemist at (7, 1).

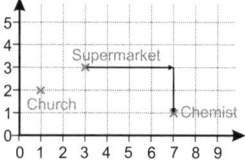

12) 32
There are 5 fifths in 1, so in 6 there are 6 × 5 = 30 fifths. So in 6$\frac{2}{5}$ there are 30 + 2 = 32 fifths.

13) E
An easy way to count back in steps of 9 is to take away 10 and then add 1. The numbers Halima will count are 39, 30, 21, 12, 3. So 3 is the number from the options she will count. This is answer E.

14) A
There are 2 drinks that have banana in (Pink Fizz and Redberry punch). There are 5 drinks on the menu in total. So the ratio is 2:5.

15) 98.82
One way to work out the answer is to split the 0.18 up into 0.10 and 0.08.
99 − 0.10 = 98.90, 98.90 − 0.08 = 98.82
So 99 − 0.18 = 98.82.

16) C
There are 20 squares in total. 5 of the squares are shaded, so the fraction of the shape that is shaded is $\frac{5}{20}$. If you divide the numbers on the top and the bottom of the fraction by 5, this simplifies to $\frac{1}{4}$. So the answer is C.

17) £1.44
The cost of 4 chocolate bars is 4 × 89p. Split the 89p into 80p and 9p and multiply each part by 4:
4 × 80 = 320. 4 × 9 = 36.
So 4 × 89 = 320 + 36 = 356p.
So the four chocolate bars cost £3.56.
If Lucy pays with a £5 note, she will get £5.00 − £3.56 in change. Counting up from £3.56:
£3.56 + 4p = £3.60, £3.60 + 40p = £4.00
£4.00 + £1.00 = £5.00.
So Lucy will get 4p + 40p + £1.00 = £1.44 in change.

18) 12
The total area of Orla's garden is 8 × 6 = 48 m^2. The area of each roll of turf is 4 × 1 = 4 m^2. So, to cover the whole garden in turf Orla needs to buy 48 ÷ 4 = 12 rolls of turf.

19) £12
The total of the prices is £12.50 + £13 + £10 + £15 + £9.50 = £60. To find the mean, divide this by the number of prices (= 5). So the mean price is £60 ÷ 5 = £12.

20) C
Start by converting the fractions into decimals. $\frac{1}{5}$ is the same as 0.2, so 1$\frac{1}{5}$ is the same as 1.2. $\frac{1}{4}$ is the same as 0.25, so 1$\frac{1}{4}$ is the same as 1.25. Then compare the five decimal numbers. They all have 1 unit, so look at the number of tenths. C (1.05) is the only number with no tenths, so this must be the smallest.

21) 16
25% is $\frac{1}{4}$. If $\frac{1}{4}$ of the cars are red and there are four red cars, the total number of cars must 4 × 4 = 16.

22) E
The shape in the shaded box needs to have at least two equal sides and obtuse angles. Squares and rectangles have 4 equal sides but no obtuse angles. An equilateral triangle has 3 equal sides but no obtuse angles and a right-angled triangle has no obtuse angles. A parallelogram has 2 pairs of equal sides and 2 equal obtuse angles, so this is the correct answer.

23) £5.70
Each time Mrs Jones goes to the cinema before 6 pm, she saves £5.45 − £3.55. Counting up from £3.55:
£3.55 + 5p = £3.60, £3.60 + 40p = £4.00
£4.00 + £1.45 = £5.45
So Mrs Jones saves £1.45 + 40p + 5p = £1.90 each time. She goes to the cinema 3 times in a month, so in total she will save 3 × £1.90. £1.90 is only 10p less than £2, so 3 × £1.90 = 3 × £2.00 − 30p.
3 × £2.00 = £6.00. £6.00 − 30p = £5.70.
So Mrs Jones will save £5.70 per month.

24) E
A number that is divisible by 5 ends in 0 or 5. A number that is divisible by 3 has digits that add up to a number which is divisible by 3. So the numbers in the poster that are divisible by 5 are 75, 25 and 135. 7 + 5 = 12 (3 × 4 = 12) and
1 + 3 + 5 = 9 (3 × 3 = 9) so 75 and 135 are also divisible by 3, so the answer is E.

25) 30
Add all the numbers of children in the table together:
8 + 6 + 4 + 2 + 1 + 12 = 33. But three children have two pets, so these have been counted twice. Take 3 from 33 to find the number of children in the class. 33 − 3 = 30.

26) 35 miles per gallon
The fuel consumption is 15 km per litre, so find 15 km per litre on the y-axis, then move straight across until you reach the line. Then drop down in a straight line to the x-axis and read off the value. This is 35 miles per gallon.

27) £38.40
It costs Andrew 52p to make each scone, so he makes £1 − 52p = 48p profit on each scone. He sells 80 scones, so he makes 80 × 48p profit. Partition 48 into 8 + 6 and multiply each part by 80 separately. 80 × 8 = 640, 640 × 6 = 3840
There are 100 p in £1, so 3840p is £38.40.

28) 134 g
There are 1000 g in a kg, so in 1 kg, there are 1000 ÷ 100 = 10 lots of 100 g. From the table, there are 13.4 g of carbohydrate in 100 g, so in 1 kg there will be 13.4 × 10 = 134 g.

29) 128
The rule is to double the previous number each time. So the fifth number in the sequence will be 32 × 2 = 64 and the sixth number in the sequence will be 64 × 2 = 128.

30) 24°
The angles in a triangle add up to 180°. So the unknown angle must be 180 − 120 − 36 = 60 − 36 = 24°.

31) B
Compare the prices by working out the cost per litre.
A: There are 4 lots of 250 ml in 1 litre, so the cost per litre is £1 × 4 = £4.
B: The cost per litre is £3.
C: The cost per litre is £6.50 ÷ 2 = £3.25.
D: There are 2 lots of 500 ml in 1 litre, so the cost per litre is £2 × 2 = £4.
E: There are 5 lots of 200 ml in 1 litre, so the cost per litre is 80p × 5 = 400p. 400p = £4.
The 1 l bottle has the lowest cost per litre, so this is the best value bottle.

32) 60
You know what 5% of the number of sweets is, and you want to find the total number, which is 100%. You can get from 5% to 100% in easy steps: 5% = 3 sweets, and 10% is 2 × 5%, so 10% = 3 × 2 = 6 sweets. 100% is 10 × 10%, so 100% = 10 × 6 = 60 sweets.

33) C
There are 360° in a full circle, so there are 90° in $\frac{1}{4}$ of a circle (360 ÷ 4 = 90). A 90° sector would take up $\frac{1}{4}$ of the day, so it would take up 24 ÷ 4 = 6 hours. The angle for the time that Sunita spent running is 45°. 45° is half of 90° (90 ÷ 2 = 45), so the time that Sunita spent running is 6 ÷ 2 = 3 hours.
This is answer C.

34) 900 cm³
Each book has a volume of 20 × 9 × 0.5 cm³. 20 × 0.5 = 10. 10 × 9 = 90. So each book has a volume of 90 cm³. 10 books fit into the box exactly, so the volume of the box must be 90 × 10 = 900 cm³.

35) D
From the bar chart, 10 children travel by car, 4 travel by bike, 8 walk and 8 take the bus. In total there are 10 + 4 + 8 + 8 = 30 children. So the fraction of children that travel by car is $\frac{10}{30}$. If you divide the numerator and the denominator by 10, this simplifies to $\frac{1}{3}$.

36) £12.98
There are 5 family members who each eat 2 sandwiches per day, so the family eats 2 × 5 = 10 sandwiches per day. Each sandwich contains 40 g of chicken, so the family will eat 10 × 40 = 400 g of chicken per day. Over 5 days the family will eat 400 × 5 = 2000 g of chicken. There are 1000 g in 1 kg, so 2000 g is 2 kg of chicken. 1 kg of chicken costs £6.49, so 2 kg costs 2 × £6.49 = £12.98.

37) D
Add all the lengths together: 2 + 3 + 2 + 2 + 2 + 4 = 15 mins.
There are 6 songs in all so divide by 6 to find the mean.
15 ÷ 6 = 2.5, so the mean length of the songs is 2.5 minutes.

38) A
The distance between Paris and Nice in kilometres is 600 × 1.6. You can estimate the answer by rounding 1.6 down to 1.5. Partition 1.5 into 1 and 0.5, and multiply each part by 600.
600 × 1 = 600
600 × 0.5 = 300
600 + 300 = 900
You know the answer is around 900 km and as you rounded down, you have underestimated the answer. The closest answer option above 900 km is 1000 km so option A is the correct answer.

39) 26 488
28 is half of 56, so 946 × 28 will be half of 56 × 946.
Half of 56 × 946 = 52 976 ÷ 2 = 26 488 (see below).

```
       2 6 4 8 8
    2 | 5 ¹2 ⁹7 ¹6
```

40) E
The booking charge is £12 which you only pay once. Then you pay £2 per mile — the charge for y miles at £2 per mile is £$2y$.
So the total cost in pounds is $12 + 2y$. This is answer E.

Progress Chart

Use this chart to keep track of your scores for the <u>Assessment Tests</u>.

You can do each test more than once — download mark sheets from <u>cgpbooks.co.uk/11plus/answer-sheets</u> or scan the QR code on the right.

	First Go	**Second Go**	**Third Go**
Test 1	Date: Score:	Date: Score:	Date: Score:
Test 2	Date: Score:	Date: Score:	Date: Score:
Test 3	Date: Score:	Date: Score:	Date: Score:
Test 4	Date: Score:	Date: Score:	Date: Score:
Test 5	Date: Score:	Date: Score:	Date: Score:

Look back at your scores once you've done all the <u>Assessment Tests</u>.
Each test is out of <u>40 marks</u>.

Work out which kind of mark you scored most often:

0-24 marks — Go back to <u>basics</u> and work on your <u>question technique</u>.

25-33 marks — You're nearly there — go back over the questions you found <u>tricky</u>.

34-40 marks — You're a <u>Maths star</u>. Go on to <u>Practice Book Age 10-11</u>.